MASTERING WORKPLACE SKILLS: GRAMMAR FUNDAMENTALS

NEW YORK

Copyright © 2015 LearningExpress, LLC.

All rights reserved under International and Pan American Copyright Conventions.
Published in the United States by LearningExpress, LLC, New York.

Cataloging-in-Publication Data is on file with the Library of Congress.

Printed in the United States of America

9 8 7 6 5 4 3 2 1

First Edition

ISBN 978-1-61103-017-4

For information on LearningExpress, other LearningExpress products, or bulk
sales, please write to us at:
  80 Broad Street
  4th Floor
  New York, NY 10004

Or visit us at:
  www.learningexpressllc.com

CONTENTS

CONTENTS

Introduction

You can have brilliant ideas, but if you can't get them across, your ideas won't get you anywhere.

> —Lee Iacocca, American businessman and auto industry executive

You got the job! You made it through the interviews and want to get a running start in your new career. Or maybe you've been at your current job for a while and want to move up to the next level. But how can you do that?

One of the easiest ways to give your job skills an upgrade is by improving your grammar skills—a change that will be reflected in the emails you send to your manager, the discussions you have with customers, and the presentations you deliver in front of your team. No matter your education level, speaking and writing in a clear, grammatically correct way tells others that you are a polished, educated professional who takes pride in your work and deserves to be listened to. Making embarrassing grammar errors, however, can give the opposite impression—of sloppiness, lack of effort, and unprofessionalism, even if you are a dedicated worker. And in the age of email, your language skills, or blunders, are constantly on display.

In the 21st century, e-mail is the beating heart of most workplaces. It's how we communicate ideas, information, and plans. It connects people both inside the office and out in the world and provides a constantly updated, digital record of our daily work lives. Chances are that e-mail is the most common form of communication at your workplace, and if you work from home or for a company with multiple locations, it's even more crucial—putting you in touch with colleagues, clients, vendors, and others when you can't be in the same room—or time zone—with them.

Other forms of written communication are also key. Throughout your career, you'll want the language skills to write a convincing PowerPoint presentation, an accurate report, an impressive LinkedIn profile, or a spot-on resume and cover letter.

All of these types of communication are opportunities for you to develop and show your personal work brand: your ideas, your personality, and your skills. As with any branding, you want this to be strong and effective. That means presenting your thoughts as clearly and professionally as possible—and the first step to doing that is to make sure your grammar is sound.

This is not to say that all workplace communication is perfect all of the time. After all, everyone makes occasional typos, right? That's true, but if your colleagues can't understand your writing, or they see many mistakes, it can undercut your message—and your reputation. Your name is on that e-mail, that memo, or that handout in the important meeting. Whether you are writing a casual note to a coworker or a report for your manager, you want the attention to be on your voice, not on mistakes. To help you put that best grammar foot forward and communicate effectively, this guide is designed to review English grammar basics. We'll explain the crucial rules to learn, mistakes to avoid, and strategies for improving your professional writing. Practice exercises will help you build your confidence in your new (or remembered!) skills. Brushing up on these skills and knowing the rules behind the language will help you communicate with confidence and achieve your goals—both in and out of the workplace.

Let's get started!

PRETEST

Before you start building your grammar skills, get an idea of how much you already know and how much you need to learn by taking the pretest that follows. Naturally, the pretest cannot cover every single concept or rule explained in the lessons ahead, so even if you answer all of the questions correctly, it is almost guaranteed that you will find a few things in the book you did not already know. If you get lots of questions wrong, do not worry—this book will teach you how to improve your grammar and writing, step by step.

Take as much time as you need to finish the test. When you're done, check your answers against the answer key that follows the test. If you get a high score, you may be able to spend less time with this book than you originally planned. If you get a low score, you may need to spend more time on particular areas or on general review. Good luck!

Pretest

1. In the list below, singular words are rewritten as plural words, but not all of them are rewritten correctly. Circle the words that were made plural correctly.

basis → bases

accuracy → accuracies

diagnosis → diagnosises

fax → faxs

deer → deer

beer → beers

wish → wishs

stimulus → stimuli

chief of state → chief of states

knife → knives

knight → knightes

supply → supplies

series → series

hero → heroes

2. Circle the words that were made possessive correctly.

girl → girl's

boys → boy's

children → childrens'

Congress → Congress's

FedEx → FedExes'

companies → companie's

manager → manager's

suppliers → suppliers'

Obama → Obama's

Clintons → Clinton's

Kennedys → Kennedies'

Dallas → Dallas's

3. In each sentence, replace the underlined word with the appropriate pronoun. For example:

> *Question:*   Mary is <u>John's</u> boss.
>
>   Mary is _____ boss.
>
> *Answer:*   Mary is _<u>his</u>_ boss.

<u>José and Jeff</u> won't be in the office on Monday.

_____ won't be in the office on Monday.

I gave the fax to <u>Laura</u>.

I gave the fax to _____.

<u>The company</u> was sold in 2013.

_____ was sold in 2013.

<u>Steve and I</u> went to the conference together.

_____ went to the conference together.

Cynthia was asked to design <u>the sports teams'</u> logos.

Cynthia was asked to design _____ logos.

4. Circle the action verbs.

wash	be	hold	is
would	buy	pray	gnaw
put	write	loan	marry

5. Circle the regular verbs and underline the irregular verbs.

forgive	grow	buy	walk
wash	hide	sew	put
sit	hear	play	throw

6. Circle the correct form of lay/lie in each sentence.

Joy found her hairbrush (laying, lying) in the suitcase.

The swing has (lain, laid) broken behind the shed for two years.

The boy had (laid, lain) awake before getting up to play.

7. Circle the correct form of sit/set in each sentence.

The class (set, sat) patiently as the teacher took attendance.

Claudia's aunt (sits, sets) the table while Gert cooks dinner.

(Setting, Sitting) on the porch on a cool summer night is the best.

8. Circle the correct verb in each sentence.

Sandy carefully (hanged, hung) her new curtains on the window.

Peter tried to (accept, except) Jim's explanation, but it was difficult.

You (can, may) take another glass of lemonade if you like.

9. Add either *a* or *an* before the words below.

___ house	___ elephant
___ unicorn	___ yellow flower
___ one-way street	___ honor
___ underdog	___ loafer
___ unopened gift	___ orange
___ hour	___ occasion
___ wrist	___ admirer
___ upper level	

10. Determine which adjective best completes each sentence.

Terry's (most high, highest) jump in the high jump was four feet, six inches.

Sean's bank account was (larger, more large) than mine.

Barbara was (best, better) at chess than her roommate Natalie.

11. Circle the correct form of the adverb in the following sentences.

Joel was (less, least) active during the winter than during the summer.

The store brand's price was the (low, lower, lowest) of the three brands.

This was the (long, longer, longest) day of the year.

12. Identify the prepositional phrases in the following sentences.

Ferdinand Magellan was the first explorer to sail around the world.

Without a doubt, regular exercise is necessary for good health.

The little monkey ran around Mom's living room and climbed up the drapes.

13. Rewrite each sentence so that the misplaced modifiers are properly placed.

The woman was walking her dog with hair curlers.

Walking along the shore the sand burned my feet.

Tina bought a guinea pig for her brother they call Butterscotch.

14. Identify the verb that correctly agrees with the subject in each sentence.

Patty (fly, flies) frequently for work.

All of us (watch, watches) out for one another.

Nobody (want, wants) to play croquet in the the backyard with me.

15. Identify the verb that correctly completes the following sentences.

Neither Jessica nor Marty (like, likes) to do the laundry.

Spaghetti and meatballs (is, are) my favorite Italian meal.

Sally or Zach (is, are) probably going to be the valedictorian this year.

16. Circle the verb that agrees with the pronoun in each sentence.

Everyone (need, needs) to get any homework I assign in on time!

I hope somebody (taste, tastes) this lasagna before I serve it to see if it's okay.

Many (stop, stops) by my office to get directions to your cubicle.

17. Add the pronoun that best fits in each sentence.

The boys took _____ time walking home from school.

Nobody saw _____ name on the cast list.

The scared joey hopped to _____ mother for security.

18. Determine whether each group of words is an independent clause or a subordinate clause.

>If it doesn't rain
>We plan to go
>Take that back
>Because I overslept
>Cover your mouth
>Remember her birthday

19. Identify the simple, compound, complex, and compound-complex sentences.
>**a.** We can go to dinner now or we can go after the concert.
>**b.** When the judge announced the winner, the audience clapped loudly, and they gave him a standing ovation.
>**c.** All of the graduates will receive a degree.
>**d.** If you try harder, you will certainly achieve success.

20. Add punctuation where necessary in the following sentences.

>Although Ms Murphy has been my supervisor for four years she's been working out of the Chicago office since January 2014 so I hardly ever see her face to face
>During his meeting with Human Resources John asked Does the company match 401K contributions
>If you ask my dad who was a salesman for 45 years it's always better to talk to potential customers in person

21. Correctly place quotation marks, commas, and end marks in the following sentences.

>Why do we need to know how to add or subtract fractions anyway Chris asked Mr. Bowen the math teacher
>Im glad you came to the beach with me my cousin whispered because without you I couldnt make the most awesome sand castle and win the contest

Answers

1. The correct answers are circled below:

basis → bases   stimulus → stimuli
accuracy → accuracies chief of state → chief of states
diagnosis → diagnosises knife → knives
fax → faxs   knight → knightes
deer → deer   supply → supplies
beer → beers   series → series
wish → wishs   hero → heroes

Here are the correct plural forms of the remaining words:

diagnosis → **diagnoses**

fax → **faxes**

wish → **wishes**

chief of state → **chiefs of state**

knight → **knights** (Lesson 1)

2. The correct answers are circled below:

girl → girl's   manager → manager's
boys → boy's   suppliers → suppliers'
children → childrens' Obama → Obama's
Congress → Congress's Clintons → Clinton's
FedEx → FedExes' Kennedys → Kennedies'
companies → companie's Dallas → Dallas's

Here are the correct possessive forms of the remaining words:

boys → **boys'**

children → **children's**

FedEx → **FedEx's**

companies → **companies'**

Clintons → **Clintons'**

Kennedys → **Kennedys'** (Lesson 1)

3. The correct answers are below:
   They won't be in the office on Monday.
   I gave the fax to _her_.
   _It_ was sold in 2013.
   _We_ went to the conference together.
   Cynthia was asked to design _their_ logos. (Lesson 2)

4. The action verbs are _wash, hold, buy, pray, gnaw, put, write, loan,_ and _marry_. These are all verbs that indicate activity. You can wash a car, hold a baby, buy a present, pray a prayer, gnaw a carrot stick, put an object on a table, write a letter, loan some money, and marry your sweetheart. _Be_ and _would_ are verbs, but they are linking or helping verbs, which indicate a condition or tell you more about the other parts of a sentence—they need additional words to complete a thought. To _be_ is a state, not an action. You can't _would_, but you would get to the mall early. (Lesson 3)

5. The regular verbs are _walk, wash,_ and _play_. The irregular verbs are _forgive, grow, buy, hide, sew, put, sit, hear,_ and _throw_. Regular verbs follow a standard pattern when used in the past tense (for example, adding an -_ed_: _walked, washed,_ and _played_). Irregular verbs are words that do not follow such a pattern. _Forgive_ becomes _forgave, grow_ becomes _grew, buy_ becomes _bought, hide_ becomes _hid, put_ remains _put, sit_ becomes _sat, hear_ becomes _heard,_ and _throw_ becomes _threw_. Although _sew_ adds -_ed_ in the past tense, the past participle is _sewn_ (irregular). You should start to familiarize yourself with the irregular verbs, and remember how their past tenses work—memorization is the key. (Lesson 3)

6. The correct answers are _lying, lain,_ and _lain_. When objects have been resting somewhere, as with Joy's hairbrush, go with forms of _lie_. When people/objects are being placed somewhere, go with _lay_ and its participles. (Lesson 3)

7. The correct answers are *sat*, *sets*, and *sitting*. To *sit* means to *be seated* or *be situated* in a particular place, as the students are arranged in class, and the narrator is situated on the porch. To set means to place objects, like putting plates and silverware on a table. (Lesson 3)

8. The correct answers are *hung*, *accept*, and *may*. The verb *to hang* is a tricky one—when one is referring to a person going to the gallows for a crime, go with the regular past participle *hanged*. But in most other cases (hanging objects, hanging around, etc.), *to hang* becomes an irregular verb, and you should use *hung*. To *accept* means to approve/agree, while *except* is a preposition or conjunction that means unless. Looking at the context of the sentence, Peter is evaluating Jim's explanation, which makes approve/agree a more likely option. For the last sentence, look at what is being said. Presumably, the person has the ability to take another glass of lemonade. However, *if you like* tells you that the speaker is really giving permission. When it's an issue of permission over ability, go with *may*. (Lesson 3)

9. The correct answers are:

a house   *an* elephant

a unicorn   *a* yellow flower

a one-way street *an* honor

an underdog   *a* loafer

an unopened gift *an* orange

an hour   *an* occasion

a wrist   *an* admirer

an upper level

The best way to determine indefinite articles is to sound out the words. Words that start with a vowel sound (like *underdog*, *honor*, or *elephant*) call for *an*. Words that start with a consonant—or even just sound like they start with a consonant, like the *w* sound of *one*—call for *a*. (Lesson 5)

10. The correct answers are *highest*, *larger*, and *better*. When it comes to comparatives and superlatives, adjectives that are one syllable (like *high*) generally take an *-er* ending (for comparatives when only two things are being compared), or an *-est* ending (for superlatives when more than two things are being compared). (Lesson 5)

11. The correct answers are *less*, *lowest*, and *longest*. If two items are being compared (as with winter and summer in the first sentence), choose the comparative adverb (*less*). When more than two items are being compared (as with the three brands in the second sentence and all of the days of the year in the third sentence), choose the superlative (*lowest*, *longest*). (Lesson 5)

12. The prepositional phrases are *around the world, without a doubt, for good health, around Mom's living room,* and *up the drapes.* To find prepositional phrases, you should familiarize yourself with the common prepositions (Lesson 9). Then, when you see one of them in a sentence followed by a noun or noun phrase, you know it's a prepositional phrase. In these sentences, the key words are *around* (followed by the noun *world*), *without* (followed by the noun *doubt*), *for* (followed by the noun *health*), *around* (followed by the noun *living room*), and *up* (followed by the noun *drapes*). (Lesson 6)

13. The correct answers are:

The woman with hair curlers was walking her dog.
The sand burned my feet while I was walking along the shore.
Tina bought a guinea pig they call Butterscotch for her brother.

In the first sentence, you need to make clear that it was the woman (and not her dog!) who was wearing the hair curlers. The second sentence seems to be saying that the sand was walking. In the third sentence, who is called Butterscotch—the guinea pig or Tina's brother? By making sure that modifiers are placed next to the nouns they're modifying, you make the sentence and its meaning much clearer. (Lesson 7)

14. The correct verbs are *flies, watch,* and *wants.* Singular nouns (like *Patty* and *nobody*) take singular verbs (*lies* and *wants,* respectively). Plural nouns (like *all of us*) take plural verbs (*watch*). (Lesson 8)

15. The correct verbs are *likes*, *is*, and *is*. These are a bit trickier, because you need to look more closely at the subjects. In the first sentence, you see *Jessica nor Marty*, which appears to be plural—but the *neither* at the beginning of the sentence tells you that the subject is really no one, which is singular. In the second sentence, although the subject seems like two items (*spaghetti and meatballs*), they combine to create one collective dish, which makes it a singular noun. And in the third sentence, although you see two names (*Sally* and *Zach*), they're separated by *or*—which means that the sentence is about just one of them. Sally will be the valedictorian, or Zach will be the valedictorian. Therefore, the verb needs to be singular to agree with the subject. (Lesson 8)

16. The correct verbs are *needs*, *tastes*, and *stop*. Again, you need to look closely at the subject of the sentence (which, in these cases, are indefinite pronouns). *Everyone* is singular, and takes the singular, third-person verb (*needs*). *Somebody* is singular and first-person, which means it takes the singular, first-person verb (*tastes*). *Many* [people] is plural, and requires a plural verb. (Lesson 8)

17. The correct pronouns are *their*, *his or her*, and *its*. In the first sentence, the subject *the boys* is plural and therefore calls for the plural possessive *their*. In the second sentence, the subject *nobody* is singular—but from the context of the sentence, you can't tell whether the people involved are male or female, so you should include both the male and female singular possessives: *his or her*. In the third sentence, the subject is singular, but it is an animal, so the noun takes the neutral possessive pronoun *its*. (Lesson 8)

18. The correct answers are:

If it doesn't rain: subordinate clause
We plan to go: independent clause
Take that back: independent clause
Because I overslept: subordinate clause
Cover your mouth: independent clause
Remember her birthday: independent clause

The best way to determine whether something is an independent clause is to see if it can stand as a sentence on its own. If the clause leaves you hanging (*If it doesn't rain . . . then what? Because I overslept . . . what happened?*), then it's a subordinate clause that relies on an independent clause to tell you what's going on in the sentence. Independent clauses might not give you the most information (where do we plan to go?), but they do have a clear subject (like *we* or an implied *you*) and a clear predicate (*plan, take, cover, remember*). (Lesson 9)

19. The correct answers are:

a. compound
b. compound-complex
c. simple
d. complex

Sentence **a** contains two subjects (*we* and *we*) and two predicates (*can go to dinner now* and *can go after the concert*), so it is a compound sentence. Sentence **b** contains two independent clauses (*the audience clapped loudly* and *they gave him a standing ovation*) and a subordinate clause (*when the judge announced the winner*), which makes it a compound-complex sentence. Sentence **c** has a single subject (*all of the graduates*) and a single predicate (*will receive a degree*), so it is a simple sentence. Sentence **d** has one subordinate clause (*if you try harder*) and one independent clause (*you will certainly achieve success*), so it is a complex sentence. (Lesson 11)

20. The sentences are punctuated correctly below:

> *Although Ms. Murphy has been my supervisor for four years, she's been working out of the Chicago office since January 2014, so I hardly ever see her face to face.*

> *During his meeting with Human Resources, John asked, "Does the company match 401K contributions?"*

> *If you ask my dad, who was a salesman for 45 years, it's always better to talk to potential customers in person.*

21. The correct answers are:

> *"Why do we need to know how to add or subtract fractions anyway?" Chris asked Mr. Bowen, the math teacher.*

> *"I'm glad you came to the beach with me," my cousin whispered, "because without you I couldn't make the most awesome sand castle and win the contest!"*

The most essential part of dialogue is the punctuation—without those marks, how would we know who is talking, and what he or she is saying? In the first sentence, *Chris asked* tells you that he or she is the one speaking. The comma after *Mr. Bowen* sets off a phrase describing Mr. Bowen, and there is no indication that *the math teacher* is part of the quotation. In the second sentence, *my cousin whispered* tells you that the quote is interrupted. This non-spoken part of the sentence is set off by commas, and it's important to make sure that both parts of the quote are set off by beginning and ending quotation marks.
(Lessons 12–15)

Applying Grammar Skills in the Workplace ▶

There are no secrets to success. It is the result of preparation, hard work, and learning from failure.

—Colin Powell, American four-star general and former secretary of state

Knowing Your Audience

Whenever you write anything in the workplace—whether it's as simple as an e-mail or as public as a presentation—always assume it's on display. This doesn't mean that your notes to colleagues will be tacked to the walls or that your meeting notes will be blasted to every corner of the company (although accidental "reply-all" e-mail gaffes happen all too often!). However, it does mean that you understand that the people who *are* reading your writing are all professional colleagues—not your mom, not your spouse, and not your best friend. The voice you use in all of your workplace communication shows who you are as an employee. This is likely different from the voice you use as a family member or friend in your personal life, and that's fine. Being the employee who always presents information in a clear, well-thought-out manner tells your coworkers that you are engaged and detail oriented.

This is not to say that you need to use totally formal writing at all times in the workplace. If you're summarizing information for the CEO or you're dealing with customers or outside clients, a formal tone is likely the way to go. However, for various types of communication in your office, let the situation be your guide. If you have a friendly relationship with a coworker, it may be perfectly fine to use a more conversational tone in your writing. If you're communicating with a coworker you don't know very well, it's probably a safer option to stay on the formal side. The one thing that should be consistent when you write—and speak—professionally is that you express yourself in a clear, confident way, free of clumsy wording and embarrassing grammar errors. Good grammar goes with everything—trust us!

Using Grammar to Set the Tone

Yes, having good grammar skills can help you avoid making mistakes in the workplace, but it can also help you *enhance* your communication skills. Knowing how language works gives you the tools to change up your writing based on the situation—when you need to produce short, straightforward sentences (for instance, when writing how-to instructions), complex, intricately worded statements (when explaining a difficult financial concept), or punchy, persuasive one-liners (when developing new sales material).

Writing a marketing description or a social media post? Use action verbs, short sentences, and strong punctuation to create energy.

Simplify your life! Company X will save you hours of time each week. Click here to explore.

Writing a meeting summary? Use concrete verbs ("follow up," "send," "call," etc.) to make it clear what decisions were made and what the next steps will be.

> *The design team upgrading the website for Patricia's Pancake Pans met on Monday to set a schedule for the remainder of the project.*
>
> - *Naomi will copyedit the final site text by Wednesday, June 5.*
> - *Simeon will contact Patricia by Thursday, June 6, to determine if we will continue with Design B, chosen by her publicist last week. We will meet again next Monday to finalize the site design.*
> - *Zachary will replace all dummy text with the copyedited text by Wednesday, June 12.*
> - *The final date to complete the site is Monday, June 17.*

Writing a letter to a customer? Use clear action verbs so that the reader knows what you're offering or requesting.

> *Dear Valued Patient:*
>
> *It's time for your yearly checkup! Annual physicals are important to your overall health—make your appointment soon!*
>
> *Visit us online at www.makeyourappointment.com, or call our office directly at 202-555-0114.*
>
> *We hope to hear from you soon!*
>
> *Sincerely,*
>
> *The Office of Dr. Dyer*

Writing an e-mail that will be viewed by colleagues and bosses? Use the most specific nouns, pronouns, and verbs possible to make sure your message is clear. This will show your professionalism and organization skills—things that will always impress your recipients.

> *Hello,*
>
> *Shankar has requested that we order 25 boxes of Vicki's book to give away at the conference in New Orleans next week (starting on 5/7). Gregg will be onsite to receive the delivery.*
>
> *I will order the books and confirm with Shankar. He will then contact Gregg on 5/6 to make sure all boxes were delivered.*
>
> *Please let me know if you have any questions.*
>
> *Best,*
>
> *Geoff*

Remember: your writing tone is always within your control. With good grammar, you'll have the tools to express yourself in the best way possible.

Digital Communication

Back in the old days, workplace communication was a very formal, structured process. Executives dictated letters and memos to secretaries, who used shorthand to scribble them down on a pad of paper and then type them up on a typewriter and send them through inter-office mail. If, by chance, you needed to send the document to more than one person, the process became more complicated: you'd type up the letter on special paper to create a carbon copy—the original "cc"—or retype it again and again.

These days, things are much simpler (isn't it easier to send a quick e-mail blast to everyone in your office?), but what we gain in efficiency, we lose in quality if we're not careful. Sure, it can take seconds to whip up a quick e-mail on your smartphone as you run to a meeting. But the speed also leads to things like typos, confusing wording, forgotten details, and embarrassing errrors. In the 21st century workplace, we all need to be aware that slowing down a bit before we hit "send" will make things much easier and clearer for all involved.

This is especially important when you think about how easy it is for digital messages to circulate to unintended places after they have been posted or sent. We've all heard cringe-worthy stories about how indiscreet Facebook updates or Tweets have gotten their posters (and sometimes the posters' employers) in trouble. There's a foolproof way to make sure you're not one of those unfortunate people: check *everything* before you send it out. Remember: once something has been sent digitally, there are no take backs. If it's appropriate (is it something you wouldn't mind everyone, from your dentist to your boss, seeing?) and it's grammatically sound, you're likely good to go.

Finding a trusted proofreading buddy in your office is a good idea as well—the two of you can act as a kind of last stop for each other when writing or sending important information. It can be tough to spot our own mistakes, so a fresh pair of eyes is almost always helpful. Not only can this person help you catch pesky typos missed by spell-check or fix stray commas, but he or she may also have good insight into what you're writing about.

Tips for Writing in the Workplace

With that, here are some final tips to remember when writing in the modern workplace:

1. Don't forget that your writing voice is part of your professional "brand."

2. Always know your audience.

3. Be aware that workplace writing is often public writing.

4. Digital communication can be great for connecting people instantly but damaging to writing quality if you're not careful.

5. Knowing the basics of good grammar will show your colleagues that you are engaged and detail oriented.

6. Clear communication is a key to working productively with your colleagues.

7. When in doubt, find someone to double-check your writing.

8. Don't sweat small mistakes. Everyone makes them occasionally, and once you spot them, you'll know how to fix them the next time.

9. Don't hesitate to go back and look up grammar rules if you're unsure about something you're writing.

10. You have an arsenal of grammar tools at your disposal— now is the time to learn them!

As you take your new grammar skills into the workplace, we hope that you use them with confidence. You have the power to present your ideas and information to the world in a clear, persuasive, and impressively professional way.

Section 1: Nouns and Pronouns

Never use abstract nouns when concrete ones will do. If you mean "More people died" don't say "Mortality rose."

—C. S. Lewis, British author and scholar

In workplace writing, the building blocks are the same as everyday, casual writing. The most basic building block of all is the noun—after all, where are you without the person, the place, or the thing? Conversations would be very short and very confusing, and writing would be incomplete.

Nouns identify what—or whom—you're talking about. In a professional setting, it's crucial that you make the *what* and the *whom* as specific as possible. For example, say you are working on a project with multiple people. Your project plan wouldn't be especially helpful for anyone if you haven't assigned specific people to specific tasks. Nothing would get done, because no one would know what to do! However, if you clearly identify that one of your colleagues will handle task X and your other colleague will handle task Y while you take care of task Z, you've set up the entire group for success.

Pronouns (which take the place of specific nouns) are similarly important. When they are used clearly and correctly, your reader will always know to whom you're referring. You want your colleagues to know right away what your point is. The more time they spend trying to decode an e-mail or report, the less time they have to move forward or send information back to you.

The following lessons will walk you through the various types of nouns and pronouns.

1

Nouns and Noun Usage

LESSON SUMMARY

Learn why the noun is the fundamental component of our language.

Nouns, the most basic component of English, are naming words. They help us identify the persons, places, or things we want to talk about.

In the workplace, it's important that you get your message across as clearly as possible. That means precisely identifying the *who* and the *what* you're discussing.

There are six distinct groups of nouns: common nouns, proper nouns, concrete nouns, abstract nouns, collective nouns, and compound nouns. It is important to know about nouns and their function in speaking and writing because so many other parts of speech relate to nouns.

Noun Types

Common Nouns

A **common noun** is a word that speaks of something in a general way, like *book*, *car*, and *person*. Common nouns can be written in singular form (*book*, *car*, and *person*) or plural form (*books*, *cars*, and *people*).

Proper Nouns

Unlike common nouns, **proper nouns** name a very specific person, place, or thing. One distinguishing aspect of proper nouns is that they almost always begin with a capital letter. *Catcher in the Rye*, *BMW Z4*, and *Albert Einstein* are proper nouns.

Proper nouns are easily distinguishable from common nouns by their capital letters, but be cautious. Don't assume that every word in a sentence that begins with a capital is a proper noun. Basic sentence structure dictates that every sentence must begin with a capital letter—remember that from English class? Below are just a few examples of proper nouns. You can add one more to the list—your own name!

EXAMPLES OF PROPER NOUNS BY CATEGORY	
PEOPLE	
Historical Figures	Benjamin Franklin, Cleopatra, Lewis and Clark
Actors	Audrey Hepburn, Tom Hanks, Lucille Ball
Authors	Jack London, William Shakespeare, O. Henry
Political Figures	Franklin D. Roosevelt, Hillary Clinton, Ronald Reagan
PLACES	
States	Oklahoma, Michigan, New Jersey
Planets	Saturn, Jupiter, Earth
Bodies of Water	New York Harbor, the Pacific Ocean, the Mississippi River

THINGS	
Businesses	Amtrak, Wal-Mart, Delta Airlines
Months	February, August, October
Products	Hebrew National hot dogs, Microsoft Word, Pantene shampoo

Concrete Nouns

Concrete nouns refer to anything that you encounter through your five senses: sight, hearing, taste, touch, and smell. As you can imagine, there are countless examples of this type of noun—*spaghetti, eyes, rabbit, father, toaster oven, river*—but a few workplace-related ones are *cashier, paper, bill, receipt, desk, storeroom, conveyor belt, copier machine, server,* and *warehouse.*

In workplace writing, people sometimes avoid using concrete nouns in an attempt to sound more professional, but instead their writing comes across as vague or hesitant. Incorporating concrete nouns can make your writing more direct, clear, and vivid. For example, instead of using the word *individuals,* specify exactly whom you mean: *bank tellers, customers, custodians, interns.*

Abstract Nouns

In contrast to concrete nouns—people, places, and things in the physical world—**abstract nouns** refer to concepts, emotions, beliefs and other "things" that you can't see, hear, taste, touch, or smell. Examples include *pride, love, free enterprise, degradation, reality, ego, convenience, customer service, failure, childhood, patriotism, peace,* and *speed.*

Collective Nouns

Collective nouns name people, places, and things in terms of a unit. Take a look at a list of collective nouns, and you're sure to get a few chuckles. Many are words that you probably use all the time, such as *family, pair, couple, collection, crowd, jury, class* (of students), and *band* (of musicians), or ones that you're very familiar with: a *chain* of islands, a *school* of fish, a *fleet* of airplanes. But did you know that when a few owls get together they are called a *parliament* of owls? That a group of butterflies is called a *kaleidoscope*? Or that when cats congregate they're called a *clutter* of cats?

More relevant to the workplace world, make sure you're aware that the following words are collective nouns: *group, team, staff, committee, council, public, board* (of directors), and *battery* (of tests). What this means is that although they refer to more than one person, place, or thing, these words are usually treated as singular nouns, not plural. And this means that they take singular verbs. For example:

> The <u>committee</u> **is** selecting the winner of the performance award.
> If my <u>staff</u> **makes** it through the busy season intact, I'll be very happy.
> The <u>public</u> **has** a right to know about the cancer-causing chemicals used in that product.

The same goes for proper nouns that are also collective nouns, such as *Congress* and *Senate*:

> The <u>Senate</u> **is** voting on the bill tomorrow.

While we're discussing the right verb to use with collective nouns, this would be a good time to alert you to a related mistake that many people make in workplace writing: treating plain, old singular nouns, such as *company, firm, corporation*, and *department*, as plural words and using plural verbs with them. This might "feel" right—the word *corporation*, for example, may refer to a large organization made up of many people and things—but when it comes to grammar, *corporation* is a singular noun. That means it should take singular verbs and pronouns. (We'll discuss pronouns in detail in the next chapter, but as a brief explanation now, pronouns are words that stand in for nouns. Examples include *I, she, he, it, we, they, me, him, her, their, your,* and *yourself.*)

When you discuss companies by their proper name, such as *Microsoft, Exxon,* and *General Electric,* you should also use singular verbs and pronouns. See these examples:

> **Incorrect:**
> The <u>company</u> announced that **they are** laying off five percent of **their** sales team.
> **Correct:**
> The <u>company</u> announced that **it is** laying off five percent of **its** sales team.
> **Incorrect:**
> <u>Burger King</u> unveiled **their** new menu items at the trade show.
> **Correct:**
> <u>Burger King</u> unveiled **its** new menu items at the trade show.

But let's get back to collective nouns. As we've mentioned, in most cases you will want to use singular verbs with collective nouns, but there are situations when you should break that rule. Look at this example:

> The <u>audience</u> rose to **its** feet.

This doesn't quite make sense. The audience—a group of people—does not share the same feet. This is more logical:

> The <u>audience</u> rose to **their** feet.

Here's another example:

> The <u>couple</u> looked pleased with **itself.**

Since we're discussing people, it seems strange to refer to the couple as an *it*. This makes more sense:

> The <u>couple</u> looked pleased with **themselves**.

Whenever you use collective nouns, think about whether you're highlighting the specific people (or places or things) in your writing. If you are, it may make more logical sense to use plural verbs and/or pronouns with that noun.

Practice
Circle the singular or plural words as appropriate.

1. The couple [disagrees/disagrees] about where to invest [its/their] savings.

2. General Motors [has/have] a new policy for all of [its/their] retirees.

3. The human resources department posted three new openings on [its/their] job board.

4. The whole team brought [its/their] kids to the office on Take Our Children to Work Day.

5. The jury [is/are] making [its/their] decision now.

> ⮑ **TIP**
>
> Remember, if a collective noun refers to a whole group, use a singular verb; if the noun refers to the members of the group acting as individuals, use a plural verb. If you're not sure, the general rule is to use the singular. It is almost always acceptable.

Compound Nouns

New words can be formed by combining two or more words, thus creating a compound word. **Compound nouns** can be made up of a number of speech components, including nouns, verbs, adjectives, and adverbs. Some examples of compound nouns are *motorcycle*, *onlooker*, *input*, and *washing machine*.

Compound nouns can present writers with issues regarding spelling, rather than usage. There are three ways to spell these nouns, which are made up of two or more words. The closed form refers to two words joined without any space between them, such as *bandwagon*, *newspaper*, and *skyscraper*. The open form has a space between multiple words that create one idea, like *water ski* and *stainless steel*. The hyphenated form uses hyphens (-) between the words, like *mother-in-law* and *do-gooder*.

Let's look at how some compound nouns are formed:

noun + noun	→	firefighter, police officer
noun + verb	→	carwash, milkshake, haircut
verb + noun	→	cookbook, cross-road, jump rope
adjective + noun	→	hotdog, black eye, blue jeans
adverb + noun	→	downtime, overtime, on-looker
adverb + verb	→	input, upswing, output

Be careful to distinguish between words that have different meanings as a word pair or as a compound word. The following table lists a few of the most commonly confused compound words.

WORD PAIR	MEANING	COMPOUND WORD	MEANING
all ready	completely prepared	*already*	it happened
all together	as a group	*altogether*	completely
every one	each individual	*everyone*	everybody

> ⤳ **TIP**
>
> Always check the dictionary to find out if a compound word should be hyphenated, since there are not any hard-and-fast rules. For example, *mini-mart* has a hyphen, while another *mini* compound, *miniseries*, does not!

Plurals

You can make most, but not all, nouns plural by simply adding *-s* or *-es* to the end of the word, like *printer/printers, lunch/lunches, bill/bills, kiss/kisses,* and *mall/malls*. However, the English language can be tricky. Some nouns change completely as plurals, and others do not change at all. But never fear—there are some rules to help you know how to make a singular noun plural. Read on!

MAKING SINGULAR NOUNS PLURAL

1. **Add -s to the end of most nouns to make them plural.**
   grill/grills, paper/papers, snake/snakes, razor/razors
   The plural form of nouns like these, referred to as *count nouns*, is rather predictable.

2. **Add -es to the end of nouns ending with -ch, -s, -sh, -ss, -x, and -z.**
   punch/punches, gas/gases, garlic press/garlic presses, brush/brushes, box/boxes, fez/fezes
   It would be strange to try to pronounce *dresss* or *crashs* if we didn't put an e in front of the s, which forms another syllable.

3. **Change -f, -lf, or -fe at the end of nouns to -ves.**
   leaf/leaves, half/halves, knife/knives
   Be careful; there are exceptions to this rule—for example, *chief/chiefs, giraffe/giraffes*.

4. **Change -y to -ies when the -y follows a consonant.**
   party/parties, battery/batteries, penny/pennies, baby/babies

5. **Just add an -s after a -y when the -y is preceded by a vowel.**
   guy/guys, day/days, play/plays, key/keys, boy/boys

6. **Add -es to nouns ending with an -o that follows a consonant.**
   tornado/tornadoes, potato/potatoes, echo/echoes, hero/heroes

7. **Simply add -s to nouns ending with an -o that follows another vowel.**
   patio/patios, video/videos, radio/radios
   Be careful; there are exceptions to this rule—for example, *banjo/ banjos, piano/pianos.*

8. **For hyphenated compound nouns, add an -s to the word that is changing in number.**
   president-elect/presidents-elect, brother-in-law/brothers-in-law

9. **There are no rules for pluralizing irregular nouns; you must memorize them.**
   mouse/mice, deer/deer, child/children, man/men, foot/feet, stimulus/stimuli, tooth/teeth, die/dice, louse/lice, ox/oxen

Practice

Add either *-s* or *-es* to the end of each word to make it plural.

6. television

7. roof

8. range

9. hour

10. mess

11. dispatch

12. point

13. blouse

14. inch

15. mesh

Identify the correct plural form of each of the boldfaced words.

16. **hoof** → hoofs   hooves

17. **winery** → wineries   winerys

18. **season** → seasones   seasons

19. **whim** → whims   whimes

20. **loofah** → loofahs   loofahes

21. **cookie** → cookys   cookies

22. **library** → libraries   librarys

23. **scarf** → scarfs   scarves

24. **party** → partys   parties

25. **donkey** → donkies   donkeys

26. **summary** → summaries   summarys

27. **box** → boxs   boxes

28. **lash** → lashes   lashs

29. **puzzle** → puzzlees   puzzles

30. **bayou** → bayous   bayoues

31. **buzz** → buzzes   buzzs

32. **whiff** → whives   whiffs

33. **life**   → lives   lifes

34. **nursery**   → nurserys   nurseries

35. **loaf**   → loafs   loaves

36. **gloss**   → glosss   glosses

37. **alley**   → alleys   allies

38. **battery**   → battereys   batteries

39. **staff**   → staffs   staves

40. **wolf**   → wolfes   wolves

41. **movie**   → movies   moviees

42. **DVD**   → DVDes   DVDs

43. **comedy**   → comedies   comedys

44. **blue**   → bluees   blues

45. **abyss**   → abysses   abyssies

46. **touch**   → touchs   touches

47. **mouth**   → mouthes   mouths

48. **guppy**   → guppies   guppys

49. **dish**   → dishs   dishes

50. **prophecy** → prophecies   prophecys

51. hearth	→ hearthes	hearths
52. status	→ status	statuses
53. ox	→ oxes	oxen
54. money	→ moneys	monies
55. carcass	→ carcasses	carcassi
56. scissors	→ scissors	scissores
57. lens	→ lenses	lensi
58. bus	→ busses	buses
59. death	→ deathes	deaths
60. walrus	→ walruses	walruss
61. iris	→ irisi	irises
62. potato	→ potatoes	potatos
63. axis	→ axises	axes
64. radio	→ radios	radioes
65. studio	→ studioes	studios
66. radius	→ radiuses	radii
67. mosquito	→ mosquitoes	mosquitos

68. **mother-in-law** → mothers-in-law   mother-in-laws

69. **seven-year-old** → sevens-year-old   seven-year-olds

70. **cabinetmaker** → cabinetsmaker   cabinetmakers

71. **jack-in-the-box** → jacks-in-the-box   jack-in-the-boxes

72. **president-elect** → presidents-elect   president-elects

73. **sergeant at arms** → sergeant at arms   sergeants at arms

74. **shelf** → shelves   shelfs

75. **moose** → mooses   moose

76. **goose** → geese   gooses

77. **crisis** → criseses   crises

78. **index** → indices   indexs

79. **veto** → vetos   vetoes

80. **species** → speciess   species

⇨ TIP

Dictionaries often list two plurals for a word, as with the word *cactus*: the plural is *cacti* or *cactuses*. Either spelling is acceptable, but generally, the first one listed in the dictionary is preferred.

Possessives

Possessive nouns are words that indicate ownership—something or someone belonging to something or someone else.

Singular Possessives

To change a singular noun into a possessive word, simply add an apostrophe and an *s* to the end of it. This may sound like an easy rule, but there are many types of nouns in the English language, which can confuse writers when they need to create the possessive. Make sure that each of the following examples makes sense to you:

> the computer owned by my boss → my **boss's** computer
> the filing cabinets belonging to Teri → **Teri's** filing cabinets
> the filing cabinets belonging to Thomas → **Thomas's** filing cabinets
> the dog that the family owns → the **family's** dog
> the headlights on the S.U.V. → the **S.U.V.'s** headlights
> the daughter of his neighbor → his **neighbor's** daughter
> the mayor of Dallas → **Dallas's** mayor

As you can see, the apostrophe-and-*s* ending should also be used for proper nouns, such as people's names, as well as for words that already end in –*s*.

Practice

Use the possessive to rewrite the following phrases, as we did in the examples above.

81. the contract of the vendor

82. the graduation of Sabrina

83. the price of the car

84. the front door of the house

85. the desk of the receptionist

Plural Possessives

Making a plural noun possessive is a bit different. Most plural nouns end in *s*, except for irregular nouns like *mouse/mice, child/children, man/men, deer/deer*, and so on. With a regular noun, simply add an apostrophe *after* the *s*.

> **Examples:**
> the children of her friends → her **friends'** children
> the complaints of the attorneys → the **attorneys'** complaints
> the quarterback of the Eagles → the **Eagles'** quarterback
> the stock options belonging to the vice presidents → the **vice presidents'** stock options
> the weight of the boxes → the **boxes'** weight
> the vacation house owned by the Joneses → the **Joneses'** vacation house
> the reputation of the Kardashians → the **Kardashians'** reputation

Treat an irregular noun as you would a singular noun—in other words, just add an apostrophe and an *s* to the end.

> **Examples:**
> the bathroom for women → the **women's** bathroom
> the shape of my feet → my **feet's** shape
> the tickets belonging to three people → three **people's** tickets
> clothes for children → **children's** clothes

Practice

Use the possessive to rewrite the following phrases.

86. the dictionaries of the writers

87. the calendar of the doctors

88. the parking spaces of the executives

89. the bathroom of women

90. the toys of the children

➦ TIP

When you are confronted with a singular noun ending in *s* and need to make it possessive, add -'s.

Examples:
Tess's new shoes hurt her feet, but she wore them anyway.
A **cactus's** roots absorb water rapidly.

Plurals Formed with -'s

What's a rule without an exception? There are a few instances where you may need to use an apostrophe to make a word plural. For example, you should add -'s to pluralize an abbreviation that has more than one period, such as *Ph.D.* or *M.D.*

Example:
M.D.'s and **Ph.D.'s** denote doctorates in medicine and philosophy.

Also, when you need to write an expression with words and letters that usually are not seen in the plural form—like *if, and,* or *but,* or *P* and *Q*—add *-'s* to the word or letter.

Example:

There are no **if's, and's,** or **but's** about it; she won't be going to the concert tomorrow. She should have minded her **P's** and **Q's** and been more careful.

Answers

1. The couple **disagree** about where to invest **their** savings.
2. General Motors **has** a new policy for all of **its** retirees.
3. The human resources department posted three new openings on **its** job board.
4. The whole team brought **their** kids to the office on Take Our Children to Work Day.
5. The jury **is** making **its** decision now.
6. televisions
7. roofs
8. ranges
9. hours
10. messes
11. dispatches
12. points
13. blouses
14. inches
15. meshes
16. hooves
17. wineries
18. seasons
19. whims
20. loofahs
21. cookies
22. libraries
23. scarves
24. parties
25. donkeys
26. summaries
27. boxes
28. lashes
29. puzzles
30. bayous

31. buzzes
32. whiffs
33. lives
34. nurseries
35. loaves
36. glosses
37. alleys
38. batteries
39. staffs
40. wolves
41. movies
42. DVDs
43. comedies
44. blues
45. abysses
46. touches
47. mouths
48. guppies
49. dishes
50. prophecies
51. hearths
52. statuses
53. oxen
54. moneys
55. carcasses
56. scissors
57. lenses
58. buses
59. deaths
60. walruses
61. irises
62. potatoes
63. axes
64. radios

65. studios
66. radii
67. mosquitoes
68. mothers-in-law
69. seven-year-olds
70. cabinetmakers
71. jack-in-the-boxes
72. presidents-elect
73. sergeants at arms
74. shelves
75. moose
76. geese
77. crises
78. indices
79. vetoes
80. species
81. the vendor's contract
82. Sabrina's graduation
83. the car's price
84. the house's front door
85. the receptionist's desk
86. the writers' dictionaries
87. the doctors' calendar
88. the executives' parking spaces
89. the women's bathroom
90. the children's toys

2 Pronouns

LESSON SUMMARY

A pronoun is more than "a word that takes the place of a noun." Learn about pronoun categories and cases and the importance of making them agree in *number, gender,* and *person.*

Pronouns take the place of, or refer to, a specific noun in a sentence. To use pronouns correctly, make sure they agree in gender, number, and person with the noun they are replacing or referring to (the *antecedent,* or referent noun).

Gender

The English language has three genders: masculine, feminine, and neuter. A pronoun's gender tells if it is replacing (or referring to) a masculine, feminine, or neuter noun. To refer to a male, we use *he, his*, and *him*; to a female, *she*, *her*, and *hers*; and to animals or things, *it* and *its*.

Examples:
Joseph took Wanda's car to the mechanic.
He took **her** car to the mechanic.
He took **it** to the mechanic.

In today's society, we are moving away from gender-specific titles and using more inclusive words, such as *police officer*, *firefighter*, *mail carrier*, *workers*, and *flight attendant*, rather than *policeman*, *fireman*, *mailman*, *workmen*, and *stewardess*. This is especially appropriate in the workplace, where roles may be filled by men and women. It is never correct, however, to refer to people as *it*, so the pronouns *he* and *she* must still be used when referring to a particular person.

Number

A pronoun that takes the place of or refers to a singular noun (one person, place, or thing) must be singular as well. The same applies to plural pronouns and nouns.

Examples:
If an **employee** wants to park in the hospital parking lot, then **he or she** must apply for the appropriate tag to do so.
Employees who need to renew **their** parking tags must show **their** current hospital ID cards.

Words like *anybody, anyone, everybody, everyone, each, neither,* and *nobody* are singular and take a singular pronoun:

Everybody must have **his or her** ID card validated.

To avoid awkward language, it is sometimes better to recast the sentence in the plural:

Employees must have **their** ID cards validated.

Person

English grammar has three "persons": first, second, and third. First-person pronouns like *I, me, we,* and *us* include the speaker. Second-person pronouns involve only *you, your,* and *yours.* Third-person pronouns—*he, she, it, they, them,* and so on—include everybody else.

Examples:
I went with **my** boss to the seminar.
You wouldn't have believed **your** eyes—the scenery was amazing.
Doug said **he** would take photos with **his** new camera.

Personal Pronouns

Personal pronouns can refer to the speaker or speakers (first person), to those being spoken to (second person), or to those who are spoken about (third person).

In correspondence, you should always be careful about personal pronouns, so that your readers are very clear on whom (or what) you're writing about. Knowing your personal pronouns can help you present the information as effectively as possible.

The following table shows the subjective case personal pronouns, which are pronouns used as the subject of a sentence.

SUBJECTIVE CASE PERSONAL PRONOUNS			
	FIRST PERSON	SECOND PERSON	THIRD PERSON
Singular	I	you	he, she, it
Plural	we	you	they

Objective case pronouns are used as objects (receivers of action) in a sentence. The following table shows the objective case personal pronouns.

OBJECTIVE CASE PERSONAL PRONOUNS			
	FIRST PERSON	SECOND PERSON	THIRD PERSON
Singular	me	you	him, her, it
Plural	us	you	them

The following sentences show how objective case pronouns are used.

Please give **me** the envelope to put in the mailbox.
Should I send **him** to the Phoenix conference this year?
I gave **you** the reports yesterday, remember?

Personal pronouns can also show possession—to whom something belongs. The following table shows the possessive case personal pronouns.

POSSESSIVE CASE PERSONAL PRONOUNS			
	FIRST PERSON	SECOND PERSON	THIRD PERSON
Singular	my, mine	your, yours	his, her, hers, its
Plural	our, ours	your, yours	them

The following sentences show how possessive case pronouns are used.

> This office on the left is **mine**; the one on the right is **his**. **Hers**, around the corner, is getting **its** roof replaced. **My** roof probably needs replacing soon. **Our** neighbors are getting **their** driveway repaved.

↪ TIP

Remember, *your* is a possessive pronoun and *you're* is a contraction meaning *you are*. Try not to confuse the two in *your* e-mails or other things *you're* writing!

Last, reflexive case pronouns, sometimes called *selfish* pronouns, are used to show a subject performing some kind of action upon that very same subject. Reflexive pronouns can act only as objects in a sentence, never as subjects. The following table shows the reflexive case personal pronouns.

REFLEXIVE CASE PERSONAL PRONOUNS			
	FIRST PERSON	**SECOND PERSON**	**THIRD PERSON**
Singular	myself	yourself	himself, herself, itself
Plural	ourselves	yourselves	them

The following sentences show how reflexive pronouns are used. Notice that they are used only as objects.

> He cut **himself** on the edge of the can while opening it.
> It was obvious they thought of **themselves** as experts.
> The computerized car drove **itself** during the demonstration.

Practice

Circle the correct pronoun(s) in each of the sentences below.

1. Andrew couldn't remember where (he/him) had left (he's/his) day planner.

2. Do you want to try the new Mexican restaurant or the burger place (we/ourselves) talked about last week?

3. Maria's group had trouble working together on the project because (they/them) all wanted to use (their/her) own ideas.

4. I offered to help Jerry shop for the party, but (he/him) said he could handle it (ourself/himself).

5. Before Melissa could save the document (she/her) was working on, (her/their) computer crashed and restarted (herself/itself).

6. As a child, Chris had acted in commercials, but it was something (he/him) preferred to keep to (itself/himself) as an adult.

7. The ice cream parlor was out of Alana's favorite flavor, so (she/her) had to pick a different one to replace (it/them).

8. Elton couldn't remember if (he/him) had locked the doors, so (he/him) went downstairs to check (it/them).

9. (She/Her) fed the ducks at the pond so regularly that (they/it) would walk up and take the pieces of bread right from (her/it).

10. Avery's kids are much older now than (she/they) appear in the photos—they have outgrown (her/their) toothless smiles.

Demonstrative and Relative Pronouns

The four **demonstrative pronouns**—*this, that, these,* and *those*—refer to things in relation to number and distance. These pronouns can act as a subject or an object.

DEMONSTRATIVE PRONOUNS		
	SINGULAR	**PLURAL**
Near	this	these
Far	that	those

Demonstrative pronouns look like this in sentences:

> **This** is outstanding, Jerome.
> I should take **these** and give them to Shelly.
> **Those** are his, not yours.
> I want **that** for my collection.

The **relative pronouns**—*that, which, who,* and *whom*—relate (or refer back) to another noun that precedes the pronoun in the sentence and introduce clauses that describe earlier nouns or pronouns.

> **Examples:**
> I own the boat **that** won the race.
> The man **who** drove it is my best friend, Jack.
> He is someone on **whom** I rely for skill and expertise.
> We have entered into the next race, **which** is on Friday.

Notice that *who* and *whom* refer to a person, while *which* and *that* refer to things. Use *that* to signify information that is necessary (restrictive) to the meaning of the sentence and *which* to signify information that is discretionary (nonrestrictive), in that even if it is removed, the meaning of the sentence is not altered.

Relative pronouns are often misused in conversation and in correspondence. If you can master the correct usage of *who/whom*, it will make your writing flow more smoothly.

⇨ TIP

Here's an easy way to remember whether to use *who* or *whom*: use *who* when you'd use *she* or *he* and *whom* when you'd use *her* or *him*. Examples: *Who* is calling? *She* is. To *whom* should I give the letter? To *him*!

Indefinite and Interrogative Pronouns

Indefinite pronouns refer to unspecified people, places, or things. Some indefinite pronouns are always singular, some are always plural, and others can be both, depending on what or whom they're referring to. See the following table for the classifications.

INDEFINITE PRONOUNS				
SINGULAR			PLURAL	BOTH
another	anyone	no one	both	all
anybody	anything	nobody	few	most
everyone	everybody	one	many	none
everything	nothing	someone	several	some
each	either	somebody		
something				

Here are some examples of how indefinite pronouns are used in sentences.

> **Both** of the families took their daughters camping in Jackson Hole, Wyoming.
> **Each** of the girls brought her journal with her.
> **All** of the campers are expected to keep their sites litter-free.

Interrogative pronouns are pronouns that begin questions: *who, whom, whose, which,* and *what.*

> **Examples:**
> **Who** took notes at the meeting?
> **What** is the decision on this topic?
> To **whom** does this black jacket belong?
> **Which** is the updated report?
> **Whose** is that pen on the floor over there?

When these pronouns are not acting as interrogative pronouns, they also play the roles of relative and personal pronouns in sentences.

Interrogative pronouns can help you get right to the point in your writing by directing the reader straight to the information you need.

Answers

1. he; his
2. we
3. they; their
4. he; himself
5. she; her; itself
6. he; himself
7. she; it
8. he; he; them
9. she; they; her
10. they; their

Section 2: Verbs

The two words "information" and "communication" are often used interchangeably, but they signify quite different things. Information is giving out; communication is getting through.

—Sydney J. Harris, American journalist

In the workplace, the right verbs will make your writing more dynamic. Why simply speak to customers when you can *engage* them in a discussion? Wouldn't you rather *invigorate* your team's sales performance than merely *improve* it? Verbs tell the reader what is happening (or will happen, or has happened). The right verbs can help you express ideas or talk about processes in a way that shows the reader how engaged you are in the task at hand.

Through the next lessons, you will learn how to identify the types of verbs and how to use them to the best effect no matter what you're writing or discussing.

3

Verbs and Verb Usage

LESSON SUMMARY

Some action and linking verbs look the same. Learn how to tell the difference, and get some help with helping verbs along the way.

Verbs are "doing" words that are a necessary part of any sentence. This chapter covers three types of verbs: action verbs, linking verbs, and helping verbs. As you can tell, they all "do" something!

Action Verbs

Most **action verbs** represent a visible action, one that can be seen with our eyes. For example, *type, surf, gallop, chop, row, swing,* and *punch* are action verbs.

Identifying such *doing words* in a sentence is generally easy. But some action verbs are more difficult to identify because the action is far less obvious, as in *depend, yearn, foresee, understand, consider, require, mean, remember*, and *suppose*. It is helpful to remember that *mental* verbs are action verbs too, even though they are less visible than the others.

⮑ TIP

When compiling a résumé, always use strong action verbs to describe your school and work experiences. Words like *developed, created, improved, coached, volunteered, documented*, and *achieved* catch the eye of a prospective employer.

Practice

Identify the action verbs in the following sentences.

1. She volunteers twice a week at the local homeless shelter, where she hands out blankets and warm meals for the people who come in.

2. The dog jumped several feet off the ground and caught the stick in its mouth, before running back to its owner.

3. He understood the directions but took extra time with the invoices to make sure he followed the process correctly.

4. I suppose we should interview several candidates before we make a hiring decision.

5. They brainstormed for hours, took a short break, and then headed back into the conference room.

6. His breath fogged the windows in the cold weather, making it difficult for him to see outside the car.

7. Although Sue gave very clear directions about what kind of report she wanted, the one Bruce submitted was far too short.

8. I sent the confirmation e-mail yesterday and expect to hear back from her next week.

9. Mario spent his day off playing paintball with his friends and eating pizza afterward.

10. After I drove halfway to work, I remembered that I had left my lunch on the counter at home.

11. The clock in the living room chimed every hour.

12. You need a paperclip to secure the papers.

13. Open your manual to page 15 for installation instructions.

14. Uncle Drew cast his fishing line off the edge of the pier.

15. Lexi considered Morgan to be her best friend.

Linking Verbs

Unlike the action verb, the **linking verb** expresses a state of being or a condition. Specifically, it links, or connects, a noun with an adjective or another noun in a sentence.

Example:
Nathan and Sara **are** hardworking employees.

The noun *employees* identifies or renames the compound subjects *Nathan and Sara*; *hardworking* is an adjective describing the noun *employees*; and the verb *are* links the two components together.

Example:
Collin **was** tired after his golf game.

The adjective *tired* describes the subject, Collin, and the verb *was* links the two components together.

LINKING VERBS							
am	is	are	was	were	be	being	been

Helping Verbs

Helping verbs enhance the main verb's meaning by providing more information about its tense.

A main verb may have as many as three helping verbs in front of it in a sentence.

Examples:
Martin **walked** quickly to the bus stop to avoid being late.

Martin **had walked** quickly to the bus stop to avoid being late.

Martin **must have walked** quickly to the bus stop to avoid being late.

A main verb with helping verbs is called a **verb phrase**. It is important to remember that a helping verb need not be right next to the main verb in the sentence. For instance, we could rewrite the last sentence so that the adverb *quickly* separates the helping verbs *must* and *have* from the main verb *walked*.

Example:
Martin **must have** quickly **walked** to the bus stop to avoid being late.

COMMON HELPING VERBS								
am	is	are	was	were	be	do	does	did
have	had	has	may	might	must	shall	will	can
		should	would	could	ought			

Most, but not all, verbs follow a simple and predictable pattern when expressing past action. These verbs, called **regular verbs**, can be changed from the present tense to the past tense by simply adding -*ed* or -*d*.

Example:
Those musicians **play** jazz well. But last evening, they surprised the crowd and **played** some blues.

Irregular verbs, on the other hand, do not follow any pattern when forming the past tense, so they require memorization.

Example:
We need to **cut** 10% from our operating budget this year, despite having already **cut** 10% last year.

Here, the irregular verb *cut* stays the same whether it is past or present. Some other verbs that follow suit are *cost, burst, bid, put,* and *set.*

On the following pages, you'll find a list of common irregular verbs.

COMMON IRREGULAR VERBS		
PRESENT	**PAST**	**PAST PARTICIPLE**
be	was/were	been
beat	beat	beaten
become	became	become
begin	began	begun
bite	bit	bitten
blow	blew	blown
break	broke	broken
bring	brought	brought
broadcast	broadcast	broadcast
build	built	built
buy	bought	bought
catch	caught	caught
choose	chose	chosen
come	came	come
cost	cost	cost
cut	cut	cut
do	did	done
draw	drew	drawn
drink	drank	drunk
drive	drove	driven

COMMON IRREGULAR VERBS (continued)

PRESENT	PAST	PAST PARTICIPLE
eat	ate	eaten
fall	fell	fallen
feed	fed	fed
feel	felt	felt
fight	fought	fought
find	found	found
fly	flew	flown
forbid	forbade	forbidden
forget	forgot	forgotten
forgive	forgave	forgiven
freeze	froze	frozen
get	got	gotten
give	gave	given
go	went	gone
grow	grew	grown
hang	hung	hung
have	had	had
hear	heard	heard
hide	hid	hidden
hit	hit	hit
hold	held	held
hurt	hurt	hurt
keep	kept	kept
know	knew	known
lay	laid	laid
lead	led	led
learn	learned/learnt	learned/learnt
leave	left	left
lend	lent	lent
let	let	let
lie	lay	lain
light	lit	lit

COMMON IRREGULAR VERBS (continued)

PRESENT	PAST	PAST PARTICIPLE
lose	lost	lost
make	made	made
mean	meant	meant
meet	met	met
mistake	mistook	mistaken
mow	mowed	mowed/mown
pay	paid	paid
proofread	proofread	proofread
put	put	put
quit	quit	quit
read	read	read
ride	rode	ridden
ring	rang	rung
rise	rose	risen
run	ran	run
say	said	said
see	saw	seen
seek	sought	sought
sell	sold	sold
send	sent	sent
sew	sewed	sewed/sewn
shake	shook	shaken
shave	shaved	shaved/shaven
shine	shone	shone
shoot	shot	shot
show	showed	showed/shown
shrink	shrank	shrunk
shut	shut	shut
sing	sang	sung
sink	sank	sunk
sit	sat	sat
sleep	slept	slept

COMMON IRREGULAR VERBS (continued)

PRESENT	PAST	PAST PARTICIPLE
slide	slid	slid
speak	spoke	spoken
speed	speeded/sped	speeded/sped
spend	spent	spent
spread	spread	spread
spring	sprang	sprung
stand	stood	stood
steal	stole	stolen
stick	stuck	stuck
sting	stung	stung
strike	struck	struck/stricken
strive	strove/strived	striven/strived
swear	swore	sworn
swim	swam	swum
take	took	taken
teach	taught	taught
tear	tore	torn
tell	told	told
think	thought	thought
throw	threw	thrown
understand	understood	understood
upset	upset	upset
wake	woke	woken
wear	wore	worn
weep	wept	wept
win	won	won
wind	wound	wound
write	wrote	written

TIP

If this list seems way too long to memorize, try memorizing three or four words a day and using them somewhere in conversation or e-mail during the next 24-hour period!

Practice

Determine whether the boldfaced verb in the sentence is correct. Make any necessary corrections.

16. She **is presenting** her proposal at last year's conference.

17. I am **sent** you the file you requested.

18. The power **went out** right in the middle of my favorite show.

19. Because she disagreed with the committee's decision, the president **vetoed** the new proposal.

20. The stats in the previous report were incorrect, so **I had fixed** them tomorrow.

21. After the football game, I **had lose** my voice because I cheered so much.

22. When he called me "Karen," I realized he **was mistook** me for someone else.

23. He bragged so much about winning the board game that none of us **will been** in a hurry to play with him again.

24. Someone **leaving** copies sitting on the copy machine for nearly six hours.

25. The party **broke up** after the neighbors complained about the noise and loud music.

Problem Verbs

Conjugating irregular verbs can be a bit challenging. But there are two pairs of irregular verbs that present an additional challenge because they sound alike, even though they do not mean the same thing: *lay/lie* and *set/sit*.

LAY OR LIE			
PRESENT	**PRESENT PARTICIPLE**	**PAST**	**PAST PARTICIPLE**
lay, lays	(am, is, are, was) laying	laid	(have, has) laid

To *lay* means to *place or put* an object somewhere. This object, a noun, must always follow the verb *lay*, making that noun what we call a direct object—the object that directly receives the action from the verb it follows.

Example:
Martin **laid** the blanket on the grass before **laying** the basket of delicious food on it.

PRESENT	**PRESENT PARTICIPLE**	**PAST**	**PAST PARTICIPLE**
lie, lies	(am, is, are, was) lying	lay	(have, has) lain

To *lie* means to *rest or recline* or to *be positioned*. Instead of a noun, a prepositional phrase or an adverb usually follows the verb to complete the sentence or thought.

Examples:
The large old oak tree **lies** at the edge of the field.
The cattle **have lain** in its shade for over a century.

In these sentences, the prepositional phrases *at the edge, of the field, in its shade*, and *for over a century* clarify the writer's thought.

> *Lie/lay* are intransitive verbs—they don't need to act on anything. You *lie* down now, or you *lay* down last night. Just you. But *lay/laid* are transitive verbs—they need some object to manipulate. You can *lay* a blanket on the bed—in fact, last night you *laid* one there!

Practice

In each sentence, select the correct form of the verb *lay* or *lie*.

26. When the head of state died, his body was to (lay, lie) in state for a week.

27. After spilling juice all over the floor, Justin (laid, lain) paper towels over the mess.

28. Sick with the flu, all Tracy could do was (lay, lie) still on the couch, dozing and watching television.

29. The neighbors are arguing over the giant maple tree that (lays, lies) on the line that divides their properties.

30. That pile of files has (lain, laid) there for weeks—when do you plan to put them away?

SET OR SIT

PRESENT	PRESENT PARTICIPLE	PAST	PAST PARTICIPLE
set, sets	(am, is, are, was) **setting**	set	(have, has) **set**

To *set* means to *place or put* an object somewhere. Like the verb *lay*, it must be followed by a noun.

Examples:

A harried young mother **sets** her groceries on the counter and tends to her crying son.

She **has set** a pillow on the sofa for his nap.

PRESENT	PRESENT PARTICIPLE	PAST	PAST PARTICIPLE
sit, sits	(am, is, are, was) **sitting**	sat	(have, has) **sat**

To *sit* means to *be situated* or to *be seated or resting*. Like the verb *lie*, it is usually followed by a prepositional phrase or an adverb for further clarification.

Examples:

I usually **sit** in the front row of the theater for an unobstructed view of the performance.

When I **have sat** further back, I have found that I could not see the actors well.

Practice

In each sentence, select the correct form of the verb *set* or *sit*.

31. We (set, sat) on the beach for hours, talking and watching the waves roll in and out.

32. We (set, sat) our chairs on the beach, along with the umbrella and cooler.

33. She was (sitting, setting) in the third row, but the room was so packed that I couldn't even see her in the crowd.

34. "Would you mind (sitting, setting) my glass on the table for me?" Girard asked.

35. Those stone lion statues have been (setting, sitting) outside the New York Public Library since 1911.

Other Tricky Verbs

Several other verbs need special attention in order to be used correctly.

Most likely, *accept* and *except* are often misused because they sound somewhat alike. Their meanings, however, are very different. To *accept* means to *approve*, *agree*, or *willingly receive*, whereas *except* is really a preposition or conjunction that means *excluding* or *unless*.

Example:
I would **accept** your apology for being late today, but **except** for yesterday, you have been late every day this week.

If you're still confused about whether to *except* or *accept*, remember that when you agree to, or *accept*, something, you are "**CC**-ing" eye-to-eye with someone; when you make an *exception*, you are "**X**-cluding" something in that agreement. When writing something that will be read by your colleagues, always read through what you've written and try this "CC" vs. "X" trick to make sure you're using *accept/except* correctly.

Another pair of verbs often confused in ordinary speech is *can* and *may*.

Can means having the ability to do something. When you say *Can I help you?* what you're really asking is whether you *have the ability* to help this person.

May, on the other hand, means having permission to do something. When you say *May I help you?* you are asking someone to *allow* you to help him or her.

Examples:
I **can** make some time in my schedule this afternoon.
May I help you prepare the month-end reports?

The verbs *hang* and *lie* are unusual because they can be either regular or irregular, depending on their meaning in a sentence. If *hang* refers to a thief going to the gallows, then it is a regular verb and is conjugated *hang, hanged, hanged*. But if it is used in the sense of hanging out with friends or hanging a picture on the wall, then it is an irregular verb and is conjugated *hang, hung, hung*. Similarly, when *lie* means telling an untruth, it's a regular verb, conjugated *lie, lied, lied*. When it means to recline, it is an irregular verb, which we conjugated earlier in this lesson.

Hang and *lie* may not come up in everyday workplace situations, but knowing how to recognize and use these tricky verbs will make your writing stronger.

Practice

In each sentence, select the correct verb to complete the sentence.

36. (Can, May) I offer you a cup of coffee before the meeting starts?

37. It took us two hours, but we (hung, hanged) all of the ornaments on the Christmas tree.

38. In the Old West, criminals were often (hung, hanged) for severe crimes.

39. He was finally able to (accept, except) that they weren't going to have enough time to see the Empire State Building before they left New York City.

40. Everything in the invoice is correct (accept, except) the October 14 order, which seems to be missing.

Answers

1. volunteers; hands; come
2. jumped; caught; running
3. understood; took; followed
4. interview; make
5. brainstormed; took; headed
6. fogged, making; see
7. gave; wanted; submitted
8. sent; expect; hear
9. spent; playing; eating
10. drove; remembered; left
11. chimed
12. need
13. Open
14. cast
15. considered
16. incorrect; **presented**
17. incorrect; **am sending**
18. correct
19. correct
20. incorrect; **will fix**
21. incorrect; **had lost**
22. incorrect; **was mistaking, had mistaken,** or **mistook**
23. incorrect; **will be**
24. incorrect; **left** or **has left**
25. correct
26. lie
27. laid
28. lie
29. lies
30. lain
31. sat
32. set

33. sitting

34. setting

35. sitting

36. may

37. hung

38. hanged

39. accept

40. except

4

Verb Forms and Tenses

LESSON SUMMARY

Since every sentence needs a verb, it is essential to have a basic understanding of the four verb forms so that you can use verb tenses properly. This lesson covers not only the four forms but also verb tenses from basic to perfect to progressive!

When you speak and write, verb tenses help your listeners and readers understand when in time something is happening. The tricky thing is to remember to be consistent with your verb tenses so your audience does not get confused. In order to use **verbs** properly, you need to really understand the differences between the four basic verb forms of the English language.

Verb Forms

Verb forms may look similar to tenses, but they are not. Learning the following basic forms, or principal parts, will help you use correct verb tenses later in this lesson.

Present

The **present** form of a verb is usually the first entry you find in a dictionary (e.g., *care, forgive, think*, etc.). Sometimes an *-s* is added to the end of the present form of the verb when it is used in conjunction with a singular noun: *she cares, he forgives, it thinks.*

Present Participle

The **present participle** is made by adding the suffix *-ing* to the present form; it is always accompanied by a *be* verb, which acts as a helping verb, forming what is called a **verb phrase**: *am caring, is forgiving, were thinking.* Notice that this verb form expresses action that is ongoing.

Past

The **past** form of a verb shows action or existence that has already taken place at a point in time before now (e.g., *she cared, they forgave, he thought*). Remember that all regular verbs end in *-ed* in the past tense, whereas irregular verbs end in a variety of ways.

Past Participle

The **past participle** of a verb consists of its past form, accompanied by the helping verb *have, has*, or *had* (e.g., *have cared, has forgiven, had thought*, etc.). This is true of both regular and irregular verbs.

SOME REGULAR VERB FORMS			
PRESENT	**PRESENT PARTICIPLE***	**PAST**	**PAST PARTICIPLE****
care, cares	am caring	cared	have cared
yell, yells	are yelling	yelled	have yelled

SOME IRREGULAR VERB FORMS			
PRESENT	**PRESENT PARTICIPLE***	**PAST**	**PAST PARTICIPLE****
think, thinks	was thinking	thought	has thought
grow, grows	were growing	grew	have grown

IRREGULAR VERBS WHOSE FORM DOES NOT CHANGE			
PRESENT	**PRESENT PARTICIPLE***	**PAST**	**PAST PARTICIPLE****
cost, costs	is costing	cost	has cost
put, puts	am putting	put	have put

*uses *am*, *is*, *are*, *was*, or *were* as helping verb
**uses *have*, *has*, or *had* as helping verb

Verb Tenses

All **verb tenses** are formed by utilizing one of the four principal parts of the verb. When we combine these parts with different pronouns, we can see all the different forms that a verb can take in a given tense; this is called verb conjugation.

There are three basic tenses:

Present. The present tense shows present action or action that happens on a regular basis.

> **Example:**
> He **writes** articles for a local newspaper.

Past. The past tense indicates that the action has already happened.

> **Example:**
> He **wrote** several award-winning articles.

Future. The future tense tells us that the action has not yet happened but will.

> **Example:**
> He **will write** an editorial for *Time* this month.

⮫ TIP

Use the present tense to discuss the contents of a book, e-mail, or other text, even though it was written in the past.

Practice

Choose the correct verb tense in the following sentences.

1. I will (bring, brought) my portfolio to the interview.

2. Last week Su Lin (spoke, speaking, speak) with us about her experience with the graduate business program and answered our questions about the classes.

3. A photographer will (come, has come, went) out to our office tomorrow to take pictures of the team for the company newsletter.

4. Did you (set, setting) the patient's follow-up for Tuesday at 1:00?

5. Jeremy (learned, learning, learn) that the bus comes at 7:45 sharp every day, so he needs to leave his house by 7:30 at the latest.

In addition to the three basic verb tenses—present, past, and future—a number of other tenses more precisely pinpoint the timing or progress of actions.

Present Progressive. The present progressive tense shows action that is currently in progress. The present progressive is formed by combining the present tense of the verb *be* with the present participle of a verb.

Example:
Robert and Olivia **are running** the marketing campaign for the Kitchens 'n Stuff store chain.

Past Progressive. The past progressive tense indicates that the action happened at some specific time in the past. The past progressive is formed by combining the past tense of the verb *be* with the present participle of a verb.

Example:
Jennifer **was watching** the lottery drawing on TV last night.

Future Progressive. The future progressive tense denotes that the action is continuous or will occur in the future. The future progressive is formed by combining the future tense of the verb *be* with the present participle of a verb.

Example:
Wanda **will be traveling** to Provence next winter.

Practice

Choose the correct verb tense in the following sentences.

6. We were (eating, eaten) dinner last night when the phone rang.

7. According to the itinerary, he will be (arriving, arrive, arrived) in Denver a little after 4 P.M.

8. Whitney is (marking, mark, marked) her name on her lunch in the refrigerator this week, after her yogurt went missing last week.

9. Did you know that the company is (stopped, stopping, stop) the use of nonrecycled materials in its packaging?

Present Perfect. The present perfect tense shows that the action was started in the past and continues up to the present time. The present perfect is formed by combining *have* or *has* with the past participle of a verb.

Example:
People **have used** money as a means of exchange since about 1200 BCE.

Past Perfect. The past perfect tense indicates that the action happened in the past and was completed before some other past action was begun. The past perfect is formed by combining the helping verb *had* with the past participle of a verb.

Example:
Before that, many **had bartered** for the goods they wanted with shells, livestock, and agriculture.

Future Perfect. The future perfect tense tells us that the action will start and finish in the future. The future perfect is formed by combining the helping verbs *will have, would have,* or *will have been* with the past participle of a verb.

Example:
As of 2015, the U.S. dollar **will have been used** as our national currency for about 230 years.

 TIP

When you write, pick a verb tense and stick with it. Change tenses only if there is a real change in time. Unnecessary shifts in tense can confuse readers.

Practice

Choose the correct verb tense in the following sentences.

10. By the end of the year, we will have (be, been, being) in business for more than half a century.

11. When I (baking, baked, bake) with my grandmother, I always learn something new.

12. Once I take this final exam, I will (have, has, having) completed my MBA degree.

13. Tanya is (making, made, make) handmade invitations for her wedding.

14. We (paid, pay, paying) an astronomical amount of money to see the Rolling Stones in concert, but we had so much fun that it was worth it.

15. He has (making, made, make) such a good impression in his first few months here that the managers already want to promote him to the next level.

16. In the photo, Janelle (jumps, jumped, jumping) to block the shot as Mary Anne launches the basketball toward the basket.

17. Thanks to the company's online system, I will (track, tracking, tracked) my package from the warehouse to my door.

18. Julio will (negotiating, negotiate, negotiated) with his boss for a raise, due to his strong sales performance in the past year.

19. Rumor has it that the ghost of Old Mr. Weaver has (haunt, haunted, haunting) that house on the corner for more than 50 years.

20. When Sylvia and Tyrone's cat didn't come home for two days, they (paper, papered, papering) the neighborhood with flyers and pictures of Snuffles in the hope that someone would recognize the cat and bring it home.

⤳ TIP

A grammatical error to avoid is interchanging the words *of* and *have* in writing. Consider the term *should've*, as in "I should've gone with the blue, not the green." It is a common misconception that *should of*, not *should have*, is being said, and it is then written that way. Be careful! The terms *could've* and *would've* (wrongly assumed to be *could of* and *would of*) fall into the same trap.

Answers

1. will bring
2. spoke
3. will come
4. did set
5. learned
6. were eating
7. will be arriving
8. is marking
9. is stopping
10. will have been
11. bake
12. will have completed
13. is making
14. paid
15. has made
16. jumps
17. will track
18. will negotiate
19. has haunted
20. papered

Section 3: Modifiers

A man's character may be learned from the adjectives which he habitually uses in conversation.

—Mark Twain, American author

If you're familiar with the "color commentator" in sports, you know that it's a person who provides extra opinions and information to go along with the facts of what's happening on the field. In grammar, this role is filled by "modifiers" like adjectives, adverbs, and prepositions, which give the reader more information about the basic parts of the sentence.

In workplace writing, being able to identify and use the right modifiers will add clarity and help you refine your points. Using too many descriptive modifiers can sometimes make your writing sound awkward and formal. If you can break sentences down to include just the information you need to get your point across, your points will be clearer to your colleagues or readers—and allow them to communicate effectively in return. Being familiar with modifiers gives you a foundation for making your writing more flexible: less formal for communicating directly with colleagues, more formal for official reports or other documents. You can adjust the tone and the information to go with the format or audience.

The next lessons will take you through adjectives, adverbs, prepositions, misplaced modifiers, and tricky words and phrases.

5 Adjectives and Adverbs

LESSON SUMMARY

Adjectives and adverbs let you express your thoughts in a clearer—or more colorful—way. This chapter shows you how to use them correctly and also how to avoid some of the most commonly made grammar errors (hint: they involve the possessive).

Adjectives

Adjectives give a listener or reader more specific information about a noun or pronoun. For instance, if you said the word *dress* to a group of people and asked them to imagine what that word means, each person would probably have a different image: a long black dress; a short, slinky red dress; a cheerful yellow sundress. But if instead of saying *dress*, you said *little black dress*, you would probably paint a similar image for all of your listeners.

Little and *black* are **adjectives**, a type of modifier that gives more information about a noun. They answer one of the following questions about the noun they're paired with: *What kind?* (*Friendly, robust, spiky.*) *Which one(s)?* (*This, that, these, those.*) And *How many?* (*Nine, few, many, some.*)

Adjectives can be used in a range of ways in a sentence—before a noun or after it; by itself or with a string of other adjectives. Here are three ways to use the adjectives *long* and *confusing*, each of which is correct:

> My supervisor is famous for sending emails that are **long** and **confusing**.
> My supervisor is famous for sending **long** and **confusing** emails.
> My supervisor is famous for sending **long**, **confusing** emails.

Articles

If you're a native English speaker, you probably use one type of adjective effortlessly in your everyday speech and writing: **articles**, better known as *a*, *an*, and *the*. But there is one issue related to articles that causes confusion for even skilled English speakers: when to use *a* and when to use *an*.

The best way to decide is to use your ears. The word *invoice*, for instance, begins with an initial vowel sound (short *i*), so it takes *an*. The word *ferocious*, on the other hand, begins with an initial consonant sound (*f*), so it takes *a*. But do not let the beginning letter fool you. For instance, although the word one begins with a vowel, it has an initial consonant sound (*w*), so it takes *a*, not *an*.

ADJECTIVES AND ADVERBS

Practice

Add either *a* or *an* before each term.

1. _____ hard copy

2. _____ one-time expense

3. _____ NASA scientist

4. _____ egregious error

5. _____ gnome

6. _____ underachiever

7. _____ work order

8. _____ NBA player

9. _____ IOU

10. _____ quandary

11. _____ U.S. Treasury bond

12. _____ wholesale price

13. _____ yearly appointment

14. _____ European company

15. _____ horizontal growth strategy

Proper Adjectives

Proper adjectives look like proper nouns because they are capitalized, but they are modifying nouns and therefore adjectives. The phrases *English tea*, *Wilson family*, and *Chinese yo-yo* begin with a proper adjective, each answering the question *what kind?* or *which one?* about the noun it is modifying:

What kind of tea?	English
Which family?	Wilson
What kind of yo-yo?	Chinese

Pronouns as Adjectives

A **pronoun** such as *he, she,* or *it* takes the place of a noun. If a noun can play the role of an adjective, so, too, can a pronoun. Some personal pronouns fall into the category of possessive adjectives: *my, your, his, her, its, our, their.* Take care not to confuse possessive adjectives with the possessive pronouns *mine, yours, his, hers, ours, theirs.* (You can review pronouns in Lesson 3.) While possessive pronouns can stand alone, a noun must follow a possessive adjective, which answers *which one?* about that noun.

Examples:
Ronald took **his** *lawn mower* to the repair shop.
Victoria and Charles balanced **their** *checkbook* together.
Sara cleaned **her** *room* until it sparkled.

For comparison, here are a few sentences using possessive pronouns. Notice that the object does *not* follow the pronoun.

That *lawn mower* is **his**.
Those *checkbooks* are **theirs**.
The clean *room* is **hers**.

Demonstrative Adjectives

Like possessive adjectives, **demonstrative adjectives** (*this, that, these, those*) answer *which one?* about the object, but they always appear *before* the noun being modified.

Examples:
That *client* has asked us to rewrite **that** *proposal* before Friday.
This *channel* always seems to have so many commercials.
These *flowers* are exceptionally beautiful in **that** *vase*.
Those *shoes* are so much more comfortable than **that** *pair*.

If the word *this, that, these,* or *those* is not followed by a noun but is *replacing* a noun in the sentence, it is considered a pronoun.

Examples:
This is broken.
That belongs to Shera.
These are sharp. Be careful.
Those smell rotten.

Comparative and Superlative Adjectives

In the course of writing and speaking, it is often necessary to show how one thing compares to another. We can do this with three different levels of adjectives: the positive degree, the comparative degree, and the superlative degree.

In the positive degree, a simple statement is made about the noun:

This *plan* is **good**.

In the comparative degree, a contrast is made between two nouns:

> This *plan* is good, but that *one* is **better**.

In the superlative degree, a comparison is made among more than two nouns:

> Of all the *plans* we've seen, *this* is the **best**.

Here are some rules to remember in forming comparative and superlative adjectives:

Rule 1. Add *-er* or *-est* to most one-syllable adjectives, like *small* (*smaller, smallest*) and *hot* (*hotter, hottest*). Some one-syllable adjectives are irregular, like *good* (*better, best*), *bad* (*worse, worst*), and *many* (*more, most*).

Rule 2. For adjectives of two or more syllables, use *more* or *most* to enhance the degree or *less* or *least* to decrease the degree.

Examples:
more agreeable, most agreeable; less agreeable, least agreeable
more spotted, most spotted; less spotted, least spotted

Of course, there are always exceptions. Here are some two-syllable adjectives that allow you to use *-ier* and *-iest* in the comparative degree and the superlative degree. Note that the final *-y* is changed to an *-i* before the endings are added.

Examples:
happy, happier, happiest
picky, pickier, pickiest
silly, sillier, silliest

Last, some adjectives just cannot be compared no matter how hard you try; they are called absolute adjectives or incomparables.

Consider, for instance, the word *unique*: How can anything that is already one of a kind be *more unique*? Other absolute adjectives are *favorite*, *true*, *false*, *perfect*, *round*, *square*, *free*, and *complete*.

> **➲ TIP**
>
> A simple tip: Add *more* or *most* before a long adjective—*more frightened*, *more harmonious*, *most ridiculous*, *most delectable*.

Practice

Determine which form of the adjective best completes each of the following sentences.

16. Micah's (good, better, best) sales month ever was last April.

17. His book sales were slightly (higher, highest) than his rival's.

18. The doctor told me that my cholesterol needs to be (low, lower, lowest) than it is now.

19. After six years of art classes, she is (adepter, more adept) at drawing than I am.

20. This option will save the company the (more, most) money out of the three options.

Adverbs

Adverbs are another type of modifier. Whereas adjectives modify nouns, adverbs most frequently modify verbs. Adverbs can also modify adjectives and even other adverbs.

An adverb answers four specific questions about the word it modifies:

where?	here, inside, there, across, out
when?	never, tomorrow, afterward, before, while
how?	irritatingly, swiftly, suspiciously, fervently
to what extent?	so, very, too, extremely, really

en qui midida?

Memorizing these questions will help you identify adverbs. You can also look for words that end in *-ly*, as long as you remember that not all such words are adverbs. For example, *friendly, neighborly, costly, ugly, burly, lovely,* and *cowardly* are adjectives, not adverbs.

The table that follows shows examples of how adverbs are used. The adverbs are boldfaced, and the words they modify are underlined.

ADVERBS MODIFY . . .		
Verbs	Some trains **always** <u>run</u> on time.	Margaret <u>answered</u> **quickly**.
Adjectives	a **really** <u>tough</u> professor	a **rather** <u>suspicious</u> character
Other Adverbs	spoke **so** <u>eloquently</u>	argues **very** <u>effectively</u>

Comparative Adverbs

Just as adjectives can show degrees of comparison, so can adverbs, with the words *more, most, less,* and *least* and the suffixes *-er* and *-est*. A **comparative adverb** contrasts two words; a superlative compares three or more. Follow these rules for making adverbs for comparing:

Rule 1. One-syllable adverbs use the *-er* and *-est* endings.

Example:
fast—faster—fastest

Rule 2. Two-syllable adverbs use *more* and *most* to enhance the degree, or *less* and *least* to decrease the degree.

Examples:
quickly—more quickly—most quickly
often—less often—least often

Rule 3. Irregular adverbs do not follow either form.

Examples:
well—better—best
much—more—most

⇨ TIP

Absolute adverbs—words like *all*, *every*, *completely*, and *entirely*—already refer to everything possible and therefore cannot be intensified any further. Similarly, *never* and *always*, two extremes of *when*, would be difficult to use in the comparative and superlative.

Practice

Determine which form of the adverb best completes each of the following sentences.

21. Breaking my leg was the (worse, worst, worser) pain I have ever experienced.

22. Everyone was sad to see Grandpa go home after his visit, but I think I was the (distraughtest, most distraught) of all of us.

23. Shelly bought that car because it was deemed the (safe, safer, safest) out of the ten brands in the recent survey.

24. We order lunch from Joe's Burger World (oftener, most often, more often) than we go to Andy's House of Pizzas.

25. Due to delays on the subway, several people got to the meeting late, but I got there the (latest, later, most late) of everyone.

Distinguishing between Adverbs and Adjectives

It is not unusual to encounter words that look like they are one part of speech when, in fact, they are playing the role of another.

Examples:
The bird arrived **early** and caught the worm.
The **early** bird catches the worm.

In the first sentence, *early* is an adverb modifying the verb *arrived*, answering the question *when did the bird arrive?* In the second sentence, *early* is an adjective modifying the noun *bird*, answering the question *what kind of bird is it?*

The following table gives some examples of adverbs and adjectives that share the same form. The adverbs and adjectives are bold-faced, and the words being modified are underlined.

Some adjectives and adverbs can be a bit troublesome because they appear interchangeable but are not.

ADVERBS AND ADJECTIVES THAT SHARE THE SAME FORM	
ADJECTIVE	**ADVERB**
His <u>bike</u> is **fast**.	He <u>types</u> **fast**.
The paper contained only a **straight** <u>line</u>.	You must <u>go</u> **straight** home.
Close <u>friends</u> are a treasure.	Brian and Theresa <u>sat</u> **close** together.
Marcia keeps her **daily** <u>routine</u> simple.	<u>Exercising</u> **daily** is good for your heart.
Other words that fall into this category are *high, late, far, hard, long, low, right, wrong,* and *wide*.	

Good and Well

The word *good* is always an adjective, never an adverb. *Good* means *satisfactory* or *commendable*.

> **Examples:**
> You did a **good** *job* as PR rep.
> John is such a **good** public *speaker*.

Well can be an adjective or an adverb. As an adverb, it explains *how something is done.*

> **Examples:**
> The team *worked* **well** together on this project.
> Katelyn can *swim* freestyle **well**.

As an adjective, *well* refers to someone's health.

> **Examples:**
> Julia *looked* **well** enough to come to work this morning.
> Margo *seems* **well** after the successful surgery.

Bad and Badly

Remember to use *bad* only as an adjective . . .

Examples:
That *cough* of yours sounds pretty **bad.**
The *cream* seems **bad**, so throw it out.

. . . and *badly* only as an adverb.

Examples:
The clown *performs* magic **badly.**
Andrew *behaved* **badly** at the client dinner.

Most and Almost

Most can be an adjective when it refers to an amount of something.

Examples:
Most *cars* run solely on gasoline.
It seems that **most** *owners* agreed.

Or it can be an adverb used to form the superlative degree of an adjective in a sentence.

Examples:
They were the **most** *surprised.*
This is the **most** *intelligent* dog I've ever seen.

Almost is an adverb that modifies the adjectives *every* and *all* and the adverbs *always* and *never* in a sentence. *Almost* can also be placed before a main verb as an indication of degree.

Examples:

Adjectives: Amy has **almost every** album the Beatles ever recorded.

Christian ate **almost all** the ice cream in one sitting.

Adverbs: They **almost always** participate in the annual softball game.

He **almost never** leaves without saying good-bye.

Verbs: She is **almost** finished with her painting.

⤳ TIPS

When you use adverbs correctly, they enhance your writing. But too many can become annoying. Use them only when they are really needed. In workplace writing, try to keep things simple. A few adverbs can go a long way!

Answers

1. **a** hard copy
2. **a** onetime expense
3. **a** NASA scientist
4. **an** egregious error
5. **a** gnome
6. **an** underachiever
7. **a** work order
8. **an** NBA player
9. **an** IOU
10. **a** quandary
11. **a** U.S. Treasury bond
12. **a** wholesale price
13. **a** yearly appointment
14. **a** European company
15. **a** horizontal growth strategy
16. best
17. higher
18. lower
19. more adept
20. most
21. worst
22. most distraught
23. safest
24. more often
25. latest

6

Prepositions

LESSON SUMMARY

What's an OOP and where are they found? Find out in this lesson.

Like an adverb, a **preposition** conveys a relationship, usually of time (*when*) or place (*where*), between certain words in a sentence. A **prepositional phrase** is a small group of words that begins with a preposition and ends with a noun or pronoun. The noun or pronoun at the end of the phrase is called the **object of the preposition** (OOP).

Examples:
across town
beyond the realm **of** understanding
under the guise **of** reality
upon your approval
according to the polls

COMMON PREPOSITIONS

about	above	across	after	against
along	among	around	as	at
before	behind	below	beneath	beside
between	beyond	but	by	concerning
despite	down	during	except	for
from	in	into	like	near
next	of	off	on	onto
out	outside	over	past	since
through	throughout	to	toward	under
underneath	unlike	until	up	upon
with	within	without		

The following compound prepositions are also common:

prior to	next to	on top of	because of	in addition to
in place of	according to	in front of	on account of	aside from

Practice

Identify the prepositional phrases in the following sentences.

1. At this restaurant, the waiters sing to you on your birthday.

2. Getting to the Olympics has been his goal ever since he was a little kid swimming around the shallow end of the pool.

3. The building you're looking for is around the corner, on Bleecker Street.

4. I finally found my glasses under the papers on my desk, after searching all over the office.

5. "You hit it right on the nose," she said when I guessed the answer.

6. After Jeff completes the application, Erin will interview him in Room 214.

7. We hid our canoe in the bushes and set up camp by the river.

8. Candy signed her name on the line and passed the paper across the table.

9. Without any warning, the dog dashed to the door and barked loudly.

10. The storm caused the tree in our front yard to fall against the house.

⤳ TIP

Sometimes you may come across sentences that end with prepositions. Some are grammatically correct, but others are not. You can figure out whether the sentence is correct by rewording it using the same words. If it makes sense, it is fine. But if it does not, it is grammatically incorrect.

> *Example:* Crime is something I worry about.
> *Reworded:* Something I worry about is crime.
> (Grammatically correct)
> *Example:* It is a problem I need help with.
> *Reworded:* A problem I need help with is it.
> (Grammatically incorrect)
> *Remedy:* It is a problem with which I need help.

Sometimes it is awkward to reword a sentence that ends with a preposition.

> *Example:* Indicate which person you are talking about.
> *Reworded:* Indicate about which person you are talking.
> *Example:* She brought her brushes to paint with.
> *Reworded:* She brought her brushes with which to paint.

You may have heard or been taught that a sentence should never end in a preposition. But in modern English, this rule has been relaxed to avoid awkward constructions. Now the tendency is to use your discretion in such a situation and go with what feels right.

Answers

1. at this restaurant; on your birthday
2. to the Olympics; around the shallow end; of the pool
3. around the corner; on Bleecker Street
4. under the papers; on my desk; over the office
5. on the nose
6. after Jeff completes the application; in Room 214
7. in the bushes; by the river
8. on the line; across the table
9. without any warning; to the door
10. in our front yard; against the house

⇨ TIP

Prepositional phrases may end with double nouns or pronouns, forming compound OOPs. (*I went to England and France with her and him.*)

7

Misplaced Modifiers and Tricky Words

LESSON SUMMARY
Learn to manage those bothersome squinting, split, dangling, and disruptive modifiers that rear their heads when you least expect it.

Misplaced Modifiers

When you write, you transfer what you are thinking—what you want to say—onto paper for someone else to read. You use modifiers to describe words or make their meanings more specific. You know what you mean to say, but your message can become unclear if you have **misplaced modifiers**: phrases or clauses that slip into the wrong place in your sentences.

You've heard this before in other lessons, but it applies here as well: Clear communication is key in the workplace. Misplaced or vague modifiers can confuse the point you're trying to make. For example, if you write that "I will reschedule the meeting on Monday," it's unclear to your reader(s) if you won't be rescheduling the meeting *until* Monday or if you will be rescheduling the meeting *to occur on* Monday. The differences may seem small, but it can save time and effort if your audience knows right away that you will be rescheduling the meeting to occur on Monday.

There is a simple way to prevent your modifiers from becoming misplaced: Keep them as close as possible to the words they modify.

Dangling Modifiers

A **dangling modifier** does just that: It dangles and doesn't seem to modify any word in particular.

> **Examples:**
> After burning the hamburgers, Russell opened the door
>   in his pajamas to let the smoke out.
> After burning the hamburgers in his pajamas, Russell
>   opened the door to let the smoke out.

The first sentence makes it sound as though Russell had a door in his pajamas, and the second suggests that his food was located in his pajamas—two scenarios that are very improbable!

This error is easily corrected by placing the prepositional phrase *in his pajamas* closer to the word it is modifying (*Russell*), and placing the adverb phrase *after burning the hamburgers* later in the sentence.

> **Corrected:**
> In his pajamas, Russell opened the door to let the smoke
>   out after burning the hamburgers.
> Russell, in his pajamas, opened the door to let the smoke
>   out after he burned the hamburgers.

Squinting Modifiers

A **squinting modifier** is one that's ambiguous because of its placement—it seems to describe something on either side of it.

Example:

The department head, Phyllis Anderson, told us after we wrapped up the sales meeting to order pizza for the whole group.

Did Phyllis Anderson tell us she wanted us to wrap up the meeting before ordering pizza? Or had we already finished the meeting when she told us to order pizza?

Corrected:

After we wrapped up the sales meeting, the department head, Phyllis Anderson, told us to order pizza for the whole group.

The department head, Phyllis Anderson, told us we could order pizza for the whole group after we wrapped up the sales meeting.

Disruptive Modifiers

When a modifying clause is improperly placed within a sentence, it disrupts the flow of the words.

Example:

I will not tolerate, just because you're the team leader, your disrespectful outbursts.

Corrected:

I will not tolerate your disrespectful outbursts just because you're the team leader.

Split Infinitives

The infinitive is the *to* form of a verb: for instance, *to cook, to run,* and *to purchase.* Whenever possible, avoid putting a modifier between *to* and the simple form of the verb.

Example:
My mom told me **to** never **lie.**
Corrected:
My mom told me never **to lie.**

Managing Your Modifiers

Here are a few rules to help you place modifiers correctly in a sentence.

Rule 1. Place simple adjectives before the nouns they modify.

Example:
Wearing a **navy** raincoat, the exhausted sales clerk walked home in the rain.

Rule 2. Place adjective phrases and adjective clauses after the nouns being modified.

Example:
The man at the desk over there is the receptionist.

Rule 3. Place *only, barely, just,* and *almost* before the noun or verb being modified. Their placement determines the message of your sentence.

Examples:
Only Peter has access to the safe. [*No one else but Peter has access.*]
Peter **only** has access to the safe. [*He doesn't have permission to do anything else.*]
Peter has access **only** to the safe. [*He doesn't have access to anything else.*]
Peter has access to the **only** safe. [*There is no other safe.*]

⮐ **TIP**

The most frequently misplaced modifier is the word *only*. It shows limit or contrast, and as previously shown, placing *only* next to the word it modifies will really clarify what you are trying to say.

Practice

Rewrite each sentence so that the modifiers are properly placed.

1. Beeping constantly, I was distracted by the fire alarm test.

2. I was taught to always treat people the way I want to be treated.

3. Cooking dinner, the cat ran under my feet and almost made me drop the pot roast.

4. Green and soft, I was proud of the scarf I'd knitted myself.

5. We're all packed, and ready to happily go on vacation.

Tricky Words

As you've noticed, words in the English language can be tricky. Homophones and homographs remind us that we should not only know how to spell words but also know what each word means and which spelling of a word to use!

Homonyms

Homonyms are words that are spelled and pronounced the same but have different meanings. They are often called "multiple-meaning words."

Homophones

A **homophone** is a word that is pronounced the same as another word (or words) but has a different meaning. One of the most obvious examples of homonyms are these three little words: *to, too,* and *two*. All three share the same pronunciation, but they each mean something very different.

It's easy to make a grammar or spelling mistake with homonyms if you're writing quickly or simply don't know the different spellings. Make sure you're familiar with the homonyms below, so when you use them in your (not *you're!*) writing, you choose the correct word.

HOMOPHONES	
ad/add	The **ad** drove traffic to our site. **Add** all of the invoices for November.
aisle/isle/I'll	The grocery **aisle** was messy and chaotic. They bought a small **isle** in the Gulf of Mexico. **I'll** show you how to do this.
allowed/aloud	No one is **allowed** in my office without permission. I heard him read my name **aloud** today.
ant/aunt	I saw an **ant** carry a crumb up the table leg. **Aunt** Myrtle is eccentric.
ate/eight	We **ate** all of the popcorn in the break room. There are **eight** people registered for the blood drive.
bare/bear	Old Mother Hubbard's cupboard was **bare**. **Bear** hunting is illegal in some states.

HOMOPHONES (continued)

blew/blue	Linda **blew** out her birthday candles. One **blue** sock was missing.
brake/break	Tap the **brake** gently when stopping in snow. Give me a **break**, please.
buy/by	Can you **buy** milk on your way home? They quickly ran **by** the store.
cent/scent/sent	One **cent** is called a penny. I recognized the **scent** of her perfume immediately. Greg **sent** flowers to Dahlia on Administrative Professionals Day.
chews/choose	My dog **chews** on almost anything. We need to **choose** a different font.
colonel/kernel	Grandpa Jim was a **colonel** in the Army. Don't bite down on the popcorn **kernel**.
dear/deer	She is such a **dear** friend. **Deer** roam the woods beside my house.
dew/do/due	The morning **dew** felt cold on my feet. I **do** not like licorice. The first payment is **due** in four days.
ewe/yew/you	The **ewe** watched her lamb closely. A small evergreen called a **yew** can be found on most continents. I think **you** have done a great job.
flew/flu/flue	They **flew** to Orlando for the conference. Six people are out sick with the **flu**. The chimney **flue** was dirty.
flour/flower	The bakery ordered 60 pounds of **flour**. The **flower** lasted only four days in the vase.
heal/heel/he'll	Wounds **heal** at different rates. When she took off her sandals, she noticed that she had a huge blister on her right **heel**. **He'll** be the best choice, I think.
hear/here	Can you **hear** well? **Here** are the completed forms.
hole/whole	The **hole** they dug was three feet deep. I can't believe I read the **whole** report.
hour/our	Within the next **hour**, you will see a real difference. **Our** branch is closing in September.
knew/new	He **knew** better than to do that. The **new** office will have more space than the current one.

HOMOPHONES (continued)

knot/not	I tried to untie the **knot** in his reasoning. They could **not** agree on the best course of action.
know/no	I **know** how to format the spreadsheet. **No**, now is not a good time.
meat/meet	The **meat** at her butcher shop is fresh. Let's **meet** next week to finish this.
need/kneed/ knead	I **need** a vacation; do you? Nathan got **kneed** in the side by his opponent. You must **knead** the bread dough before letting it rise.
one/won	Eileen has **one** more hour of work left. Ashley wished she had **won** the prize.
pair/pear	Worried that his new loafers would be squeaky, Steve packed an extra **pair** of shoes for the conference. I hate to sound snobby, but I prefer **pear** tart to plain, old apple pie.
peak/peek/pique	She reached the **peak** of her career in the late 1990s, but she's still regarded with respect. He took a quick **peek** in her shopping bag. What I overheard began to **pique** my curiosity.
principal/principle	The **principal** idea is to help others. It's the **principle** of the matter and nothing else.
rain/reign/rein	Will it **rain** again tomorrow? King Henry VIII's **reign** over England lasted 38 years. The horse's **rein** was worn and needed replacing.
right/rite/write	Turn **right** at the light up ahead. In the old days, working in the mailroom was considered to be a **rite** of passage. Bosses often ask employees to **write** self-reviews.
sail/sale	Jan will **sail** in the Caribbean for one week. Our fall **sale** will last until December.
scene/seen	Police officers swarmed around the **scene** of the crime. Have you **seen** my copy of the annual report?
stationary/ stationery	The guard stood **stationary** for several hours. The new **stationery** has a typo in the letterhead.
there/their/they're	**There** is a chance that we can go. It took **their** bus 18 hours to get home. **They're** supposed to confirm the appointment within 24 hours.

HOMOPHONES *(continued)*

threw/through	She accidentally **threw** away the document. I looked **through** the entire report, and there was no information about last year's earnings.
to/too/two	Please be sure **to** make two copies for the president's assistant, too. Please be sure to make two copies for the president's assistant, **too**. Please be sure to make **two** copies for the president's assistant, too.
which/witch	**Which** insurance plan you choose is solely up to you. Dorothy outsmarted the wicked **witch** in her own castle.
who's/whose	**Who's** going to Albany with Craig tomorrow? **Whose** coat is in the conference room?
wood/would	Pile the **wood** by the back of the shed. **Would** you care to give me a hand?
your/you're	Pick up **your** papers on the way out. Let me know if **you're** going to the meeting.

Homographs

Homographs are words that are spelled the same but are pronounced differently and have different meanings. Below are some familiar examples.

HOMOGRAPHS	
address	You should **address** the envelope with the **address** on the label.
bass	He is a **bass** fisherman and also plays the **bass** in a rock band.
bow	I was asked to **bow** to the king and remove my **bow** and arrows.
close	My manager will **close** up tonight; luckily he lives **close** by.
conflict	The reports about the recent **conflict** in Congress **conflict**.
desert	The soldier did not **desert** his unit in the **desert**.
does	He **does** see the **does** standing off to the side of the road.
dove	The **dove dove** toward the flock of gulls to defend his mate.
house	The **house** around the corner will **house** your dog while you're away.
lead	At the public-health conference, Dr. Brown will **lead** a seminar about the dangers of **lead** paint.
live	I **live** next to the arena, so I'll see many **live** concerts.
minute	The **minute** I saw her, she hounded me about the most **minute** details of the contract.
present	It was an honor to **present** this special **present** to the winner.
produce	The orchard didn't **produce** much fruit this year, but there was still plenty of other **produce** available at the farm stand.
read	I will **read** the same book you **read** last summer.
record	Don't forget to **record** his high-jump **record** in the books.
resume	You **resume** work on your cover letter, and I'll read through your **resume** for typos.

HOMOGRAPHS (*continued*)	
separate	**Separate** the folders by color and place them in **separate** drawers in the file cabinet.
tear	"Don't **tear** up my drawing!" the little girl said with a **tear** in her eye.
use	I don't have any **use** for that filing cabinet, so feel free to **use** it.
wind	We had to **wind** up the company picnic early because people started to complain about the **wind**.
wound	He was lucky—his truck was totaled, but he **wound** up with only a small **wound** on his left hand.

⇨ TIP

Remember to use grammar check as well as spell-check when you write. Spell-check will say this sentence is correct: "The hair hopped down the rode," because those are real words . . . but not the right ones. It should be: "The hare hopped down the road." You can also ask a friend or colleague to look over your writing. A second pair of eyes can help catch errors that your computer's spell-check might miss.

Practice

Each question provides definitions for words that are homophones (they sound alike but have different meanings and spellings). Fill in the blanks with the correct spelling of the words.

6. the top of a mountain: _____
a glimpse or quick look: _____

7. the flesh of an animal that's used for food, such as pork or beef: _____
encounter someone: _____

8. water that falls from the sky: _____
the period during which a ruler rules: _____
a thin strap attached to a horse's bit: _____

9. a smell: _____
a penny: _____

10. the person in charge of a school: _____
a fundamental truth: _____

11. a large, grizzly mammal: _____
unclothed or exposed: _____

12. the part of a car that slows it down or stops it from moving:
_____
an interruption, pause, or crack: _____

Answers

Answers for questions 1–5 are suggestions. Your answers may vary.

1. I was distracted by the fire alarm, which was beeping constantly during the test.
2. I was taught always to treat people the way I want to be treated.
3. While I was cooking dinner, the cat ran under my feet and almost made me drop the pot roast.
4. I was proud of the green, soft scarf I'd knitted myself.
5. We're all packed, and happily ready to go on vacation.
6. the top of a mountain: **peak**
   a glimpse or quick look: **peek**
7. the flesh of an animal that's used for food, such as pork or beef: **meat**
   encounter someone: **meet**
8. water that falls from the sky: **rain**
   the period during which a ruler rules: **reign**
   a thin strap attached to a horse's bit: **rein**
9. a smell: **scent**
   a penny: **cent**
10. the person in charge of a school: **principal**
    a fundamental truth: **principle**
11. a large, grizzly mammal: **bear**
    unclothed or exposed: **bare**
12. the part of a car that slows it down or stops it from moving: **brake**
    an interruption, pause, or crack: **break**

Section 4: Sentence Structure

It is my ambition to say in ten sentences what others say in a whole book.

—Friedrich Nietzsche, German philosopher

Complete, clear, well-structured sentences tell people that you care about the idea you are expressing. Brief, conversational sentence fragments might work best if you're having a casual discussion with someone or trying to show information in quick soundbites (like in a presentation). However, using full, clear sentences in e-mails or other documents is one of the most basic ways to show that you take the topic seriously.

Knowing when to change up your sentence structure is the mark of an organized writer and shows that you are invested in how you present yourself.

8

Sentence Basics and Subject-Verb Agreement

LESSON SUMMARY

To be a sentence, a group of words must express a complete idea and include a subject and a verb. In this lesson, learn what complements are and how they come into play in a well-crafted sentence. Then learn when to use singular or plural verbs in your writing.

The fundamental component of speech and writing, sentences help people communicate their ideas to others. Every complete sentence is made up of two major components: a subject—a noun or pronoun that tells *whom* or *what* the sentence is about—and a predicate—a verb that tells what the subject is *doing* or what *condition* the subject is in.

Subjects

Finding the **subject** of a sentence is as simple as asking *who?* or *what?* in relation to the verb. In the following examples, the subject is underlined once and the verb is underlined twice.

A subject can be a proper noun:

> S   V
> <u>Thomas</u> <u>updates</u> his resume regularly.

Who <u>updates</u>? Thomas; thus, <u>Thomas</u> is the subject.

A subject can be a common noun:

> S   V
> The real estate <u>market</u> <u>fluctuates</u> yearly.

What <u>fluctuates</u>? The market; thus, <u>market</u> is the subject.

A subject can be a pronoun:

> S   V
> <u>They</u> <u>traveled</u> overseas for the meeting.

Who <u>traveled</u>? They; thus, <u>They</u> is the subject.

A subject can be compound (two or more nouns playing an equal role in the sentence):

> S   S   V
> <u>Books</u> and the <u>Internet</u> <u>contain</u> helpful information.

What <u>contain</u>? Books and the Internet; thus, <u>Books</u> and <u>Internet</u> play an equal role in the compound subject.

Although the subject is typically found at the beginning of the sentence, it can also appear elsewhere.

In the middle:

$$\overset{\text{S}}{}\qquad\overset{\text{V}}{}$$

Before lunch, <u>Michelle</u> <u><u>decided</u></u> to run quickly to the bank.

At the end:

$$\overset{\text{V}}{}\qquad\qquad\overset{\text{S}}{}$$

At the end of the pier <u><u>sat</u></u> the lone <u>fisherman</u>.

Tricky Subjects

Not all sentences have an obvious, or stated, noun or pronoun as a subject; sometimes the subject is implied. Imperative sentences (sentences that make a request or a command) always have an implied subject:

<u><u>Wash</u></u> your hands frequently during the day to prevent colds.

If you ask yourself *who* or *what* <u>wash</u>, there is not a noun in the sentence that answers the question. That is because the subject is *implied*; it is the pronoun *you*:

$$\overset{\text{S}}{}\quad\overset{\text{V}}{}$$

(<u>You</u>) <u><u>wash</u></u> your hands frequently during the day to prevent colds.

To find the subject in a question, turn it into a statement that places the subject before the verb:

Did Ed go to the convention in Seattle?

becomes:

$$\overset{\text{S}}{}\quad\overset{\text{V}}{}$$

<u>Ed</u> <u><u>went</u></u> to the convention in Seattle.

You can then ask yourself *who* <u><u>went</u></u>? *Ed* is your subject.

Predicates

A **predicate** tells something about the subject or subjects in a sentence. The verb, known as the **simple predicate**, expresses the action done by or to the subject or tells about its condition. You can find the simple predicate in a sentence by asking yourself which word indicates action being done by or to the subject or conveys the condition of the subject.

Examples:

S   V
She approached her supervisor about her recent performance review.

S
The itinerary for Joseph's business trip

V
was changed.

S   V
Meghan was energetic and results-driven.

Like subjects, predicates can be single or compound, which means there are two or more verbs relating to the same subject or compound subject in the sentence.

Examples:

S   V   V   V   V
At practice, we stretch, run, drill, and scrimmage.

S   S   V
Last Monday, George and Marty arrived late and

V
ran two extra laps.

Complements

The purpose of good communication is to get your message across clearly. Sometimes a sentence has a clear message with *just* a subject and a verb:

>Stanley left.
>Please reply.
>What gives?
>Did you go?

Other sentences may require more information to complete their meaning:

>Kyle picked _____. [*What did he pick?*]
>Gina took _____. [*What did she take?*]

The additional parts that these sentences require are called **complements**.

>**Examples:**
>Kyle picked **Andrew first.**
>Gina took **a breath.**

The complements *Andrew* and *breath* complete the meaning in these sentences by telling us *what* the subjects *picked* and *took*.

Direct and Indirect Objects

A **direct object** is a complement in a sentence with an *action verb*. It is a noun or pronoun that "directly" relates to the action verb and receives action from that verb. Direct objects answer *whom?* or *what?* about the action verb.

Examples:

S   V   D.O.
Kyle picked Andrew first.   Picked whom?
                                   Andrew

S   V   D.O.
Gina took a breath.   Took what?
                                   a *breath*

Like subjects and predicates, direct objects can also be **compound**:
One or more verbs share more than one object.

Example:

S   V
Wanda, a successful real estate agent, listed and

V   D.O.   D.O.
sold a **house** and a **farm** this week.

⇨ TIP

Every sentence must have a subject, but not every sentence
will have an object.

A sentence that has a direct object can also have an **indirect object**.
It tells which person or thing is the recipient of the direct object, so
you cannot have an indirect object without a direct object. You can
easily identify an indirect object by asking yourself *to or for whom?*
or *to or for what?* after an action verb. Indirect objects are usually
placed between the verb and the direct object.

Example:

S   V   I.O.
The car salesperson showed Chris the latest

D.O.
Mustang GT model.

Predicate Nouns and Predicate Adjectives

Known as **subject complements**, predicate nouns rename the subject, and predicate adjectives describe the subject.

When a predicate noun follows a linking verb, the linking verb acts like an equals sign (=):

$$\text{DeVaughn } \underset{\text{V}}{\underline{\underline{\text{is}}}} \text{ the } \boxed{\underset{\text{P.N.}}{\text{coach}}}.$$

DeVaughn = the coach.

Predicate nouns can also be compound in form, as long as they are identifying the same noun:

$$\underset{\text{S}}{\underline{\text{Carla}}} \underset{\text{V}}{\underline{\text{was}}} \boxed{\underset{\text{P.N.}}{\text{professor}}} \text{ and } \boxed{\underset{\text{P.N.}}{\text{mentor}}} \text{ to many students.}$$

Predicate adjectives also follow a linking verb, describe or modify the subject, and can be compound in form as well:

Following the interview, $\underset{\text{S}}{\underline{\text{Bill}}} \underset{\text{V}}{\underline{\text{felt}}} \boxed{\underset{\text{P.A.}}{\text{excited}}}$ and $\boxed{\underset{\text{P.A.}}{\text{optimistic}}}$.

Remember that *complement* means "add to or complete." Predicate nouns and predicate adjectives add to or complete an idea to make it more precise or clear.

Subject-Verb Agreement

Subjects and verbs must always be compatible in number and person. A singular subject—referring to only one person, place, or

SENTENCE BASICS AND SUBJECT-VERB AGREEMENT

thing—must be coupled with a singular verb. Likewise, plural sub-jects—referring to more than one person, place, or thing—need a plural verb.

Singular:	Shirley **wants** to buy a new car. Rex usually **plays** catch with me.	She **is** shopping for one now. He **was** not feeling well today.
Plural:	Trish and Dot **run** errands together. Sandy, Alexa, and I **discuss** books.	They **are** at the supermarket. We **were** hoping to meet today.

Notice the endings of the singular and the plural verbs. Unlike nouns, third-person singular verbs end in -s, while the corresponding plural verbs do not.

Verbs move sentences along. We are able to tell *when* events happen simply by noting the verb tense in a sentence. Because many verbs are easily recognizable, they come across as exceptionally harsh to our ears if used improperly. This is especially true of the most widely used verb form in the English language, *be*. The following table shows how *be* is conjugated according to number, form, and person (singular/plural, first/second/third person).

	SUBJECT	PRESENT	PAST
First/S	I	am	was
Second/S and P	you	are	were
Third/S	he, she, it	is	was
First/P	we	are	were
Third/P	they	are	were

It is interesting to note that the conjugated forms of *be* don't include the word *be* itself. For reference, the nonparticipial forms of *be* are as follows: *am, is, are, was, were.*

130

That being said, it is not unusual to hear *be* used improperly as a verb in casual language. Remember this rule: *Be* **never** follows a subject in a sentence without a helping verb.

Incorrect:
I **be** taking the mail to the post office this morning.
They **be** cooking dinner, and we **be** washing the dishes.

Correct:
I **am** taking the mail to the post office this morning.
They **are** cooking dinner, and we **are** washing the dishes.

Practice

Identify the verb that agrees with the subject in each sentence.

1. According to the itinerary, Sheila and I (arrive, arrives) in Copenhagen around 4:00.

2. We (be, are, is) closing the office early on the day before Thanksgiving.

3. Sometimes on rainy Saturday afternoons, I (make, makes) popcorn and have a movie marathon at home.

4. The directions (tell, tells) you to unplug the power cord after the device has finished charging.

5. He and Elton (meet, meets) every Monday afternoon to have coffee and talk about Sunday's Patriots game.

6. Please note that all equipment (belong, belongs) to the township.

7. Your flight (arrive, arrives) in Denver at six o'clock.

8. The statistics (is, are) the centerpiece of my plan.

9. If we (walk, walks) quickly we can catch the 5:15 train.

10. My computer and monitor (need, needs) to be replaced.

> **⇒ TIP**
>
> Do not let long sentences confuse you. Verbs do not have to agree with words that come between the subject and verb. "Jamal, as well as his colleagues Alec and Carlos, is eligible for a promotion." The singular subject, *Jamal*, takes a singular verb, *is*.

Compound Subjects and Verbs

When two or more subjects share the same verb, you have what is called a **compound subject**. The conjunctions *and*, *or*, and *nor* are used to connect compound subjects.

Example:
White and navy blue **are** the colors of our new logo.

When *and* is used, the subjects are looked at as equals, so the verb is plural. An exception to this rule is when the subjects are thought of as a single unit, like *spaghetti and meatballs* or *macaroni and cheese*.

When singular subjects are joined by *or* or *nor*, each subject is considered a separate unit, so the verb is *singular*. When plural subjects are joined by *or* or *nor*, the verb is *plural*, since each of the subjects is plural.

Singular:

Green or yellow squash **is** used in this recipe.

Neither the chair nor the table **has** any scratches.

Plural:

Coaches or managers **attend** the monthly team meetings.

Neither parents nor spectators **have** any interest in attending.

⇨ TIP

In a sentence with a singular and a plural subject, it may be hard to decide whether to use a singular or a plural verb. But the solution is simple: Whichever subject is mentioned last in the sentence, whether singular or plural, determines the correct verb to use:

Either *pancakes* or *cereal* **is** available for breakfast today.
Either *cereal* or *pancakes* **are** available for breakfast today.

Practice

In each sentence, circle the verb that agrees with the subject.

11. Some of us in the office (take, takes) the A train, while others take the F train.

12. Neither Joe nor Mary (like, likes) seafood, so they always get chicken or salads when they go to Arnold's Crab Shack.

13. Neither Zack nor Mary (work, works) on that project.

14. Both of you (is, are) being very rude.

15. Every week Tyrone or Genevieve (meet, meets) with new clients to discuss their advertising needs.

Pronoun Subjects and Verbs

Indefinite pronouns, such as *everyone*, *both*, *few*, and *all*, are general when referring to people, places, or things. Because we are concerned with subjects and verbs agreeing in number, it is easy to tell if most indefinite pronouns are singular or plural, with only a handful of exceptions.

INDEFINITE PRONOUNS					
SINGULAR				**PLURAL**	**BOTH**
anybody	everybody	neither	other	both	all
anyone	everyone	nobody	somebody	few	any
anything	everything	no one	someone	many	more
each	little	nothing	something	others	most
either	much	one		several	none
					some

As with any other pronoun, a singular indefinite pronoun takes a singular verb, and a plural one takes a plural verb. When using pronouns that can be both singular and plural, you need to look at the noun being referred to by the indefinite pronoun to help you determine which verb to use:

> **Most** of these *peaches* **are** bruised.
> **Most** of his *room* **is** clean.

Practice

Identify the verb that agrees with the indefinite pronouns in the following sentences.

16. Most of us (is, are) not even from this town.

17. Anybody who (think, thinks) waiting tables is an easy job should spend an hour working at my restaurant.

18. Somebody (need, needs) to remind me when it's time to leave.

19. Everything (seem, seems) more fun when you have good company.

20. All of us (remember, remembers) that day when Clyde announced his resignation.

Answers

1. arrive
2. are
3. make
4. tell
5. meet
6. belongs
7. arrives
8. are
9. walk
10. need
11. take
12. likes
13. works
14. are
15. meets
16. are
17. thinks
18. needs
19. seems
20. remember

9

Phrases and Clauses

LESSON SUMMARY

Did you know that in a sentence, a little group of words can wear many hats? Well, it can. In one sentence, it may act like an adjective; in another, it may be like an adverb; and in still another, it may function as a noun. Find out how, and then learn how clauses can function as stand-alone sentences.

Phrases

A **phrase** is a group of two or more words that makes sense, but not complete sense, because it does not have both a subject and a verb. The group of words that make up a phrase—and there are many kinds of phrases—is used as a single part of speech.

SAMPLE PHRASES	
NO PREDICATE	**NO SUBJECT**
The computers	goes skating often
Several	is from another state
Our house	are missing some parts

Prepositional Phrases

The **prepositional phrase** is the most common type of phrase.

Adjective and Adverb Phrases

A prepositional phrase, which begins with a preposition and ends with a noun or pronoun, can function like an adjective or adverb in a sentence. Like an adjective, an adjective phrase answers *what kind?* or *which one?* about the noun or pronoun it modifies. Unlike an adjective, which typically precedes the noun it modifies, an adjective phrase generally comes after the noun.

> **Example:**
> A group of us **from the Accounting department** are meeting tonight for dinner.

Here, the prepositional phrase *from the Accounting department* acts like an adjective. We know it is an adjective phrase because it modifies the noun *group* and answers the question *which one?* about the group.

Adverb phrases modify verbs, adjectives, and adverbs. An adverb phrase answers *where? when? how?* or *to what extent?* about the word it modifies and usually provides more detail than a typical adverb.

Example:
We will meet **at our favorite restaurant at six o'clock**.

Here, the prepositional phrases *at our favorite restaurant* and *at six o'clock* act like adverbs, modifying the verb *meet* and answering the questions *where?* and *when?* about the meeting.

⤷ TIP

> Remember, a phrase is just a group of words. It may be a subject or a predicate, but it cannot be both. Therefore, it cannot stand alone as a sentence.

Verbal Phrases

The three types of verbal phrases are participial phrases (which act like adjectives), infinitive phrases (which act like nouns, adjectives, or adverbs), and gerund phrases (which act like nouns).

Participial Phrases

Participial phrases begin with a participle—a present tense (*-ing*) verb or a past tense (*-ed, -en, -t,* or *-n*) verb. These phrases act like adjectives, describing or giving more detail about nouns or pronouns.

Examples:
Looking hot and tired, the gardener sat in the shade of a nearby tree.
Shaken by the unexpected accident, Harry called 911 for assistance.

The present participle *looking* (*look* + *ing*) modifies the noun *gardener*. The words *hot and tired* complete the participial phrase. The phrase *shaken by the unexpected accident* follows the same configuration, except it is in past participle (*shake* + *n*) form.

Infinitive Phrases

Infinitive phrases begin with the word *to* plus a verb. These phrases act like nouns, adjectives, or adverbs, depending on their function in the sentence.

> **Example:**
> **To complete the project outline in less than two days** was Tommy's aim this week.

The infinitive phrase *to complete the project outline in less than two days* is functioning as a noun because it is the complete subject of the sentence.

> **Example:**
> Tommy aims **to complete the project outline in less than two days** this week.

In this sentence, *to complete the project outline in less than two days* also functions as a noun because it is the direct object of the verb *aims*.

> **Example:**
> **To complete the project outline in less than two days,** Tommy has cleared his schedule.

Here, *to complete the project outline in less than two days* functions as an *adjective* because it modifies the noun *Tommy*.

Example:
Tommy is clearing his schedule **to complete the project outline in less than two days**.

Now, *to complete the project outline in less than two days* functions as an adverb modifying the verb *clearing*.

Gerund Phrases

Gerund phrases begin with a gerund—an *-ing* verb acting as a noun. Gerund phrases always work like a noun in a sentence, so they can function as either subjects or objects.

Example:
Tasting chocolate for a living can be a delicious yet fattening profession.

The gerund phrase *tasting chocolate for a living* functions as a noun and is the complete subject of the sentence.

Example:
Debbie's profession is **sampling chocolate**.

The gerund phrase *sampling chocolate* functions as a noun and is the subject complement of the linking verb *is* and the subject *profession*.

Example:
Debbie enjoys **working with chocolate**.

The gerund phrase *working with chocolate* functions as a noun and is the direct object of the verb *enjoys*.

Appositive Phrases

An **appositive phrase** renames, identifies, or gives more detail about a noun or pronoun that it follows in a sentence.

> **Example:**
> My brother, **a clown by profession**, works all weekend at parties and gatherings.

In this sentence, the noun *brother* is being further identified by the appositive phrase *a clown by profession*.

TIP

Since it tells more about a noun, you can omit an appositive phrase without losing the basic idea of a sentence. In the previous sentence, drop the phrase and you still know the brother works weekends at social gatherings.

Clauses

A **clause** is also a group of words, but it differs from a phrase in that it has its own subject and verb. Therefore, some clauses function as sentences, either independently or within a larger sentence. One sentence might contain, or even be entirely composed of, as many as three or more clauses. The sentence would be a combination of two possible kinds of clauses, **independent** and **subordinate**.

TIP

> Too many simple sentences can make your conversation or writing choppy and dull. Increase listener/reader interest by adding a few clauses that supply new facts or vivid descriptions.

Independent Clauses

Sometimes referred to as a main clause, an **independent clause** can stand alone as a simple sentence.

Examples:
You have a nice smile.
It lights up your eyes.

With the help of a semicolon or a coordinating conjunction, we can join these two independent clauses to form a single sentence. (See Lesson 10 to learn about coordinating conjunctions.)

Examples:
You have a nice smile; it lights up your eyes.
You have a nice smile, **and** it lights up your eyes.

Don't confuse the comma with the semicolon. Joining the two clauses with a comma instead of a semicolon would result in what is called a comma splice.

Examples:
I looked for my lost address book, **but** I could not find it.
Charlotte watered the tree every day, **for** it was new.

Hans wanted to learn to play golf, **so** he took lessons.

As mentioned before, some sentences may contain as many as three or more independent clauses.

Example:
I looked for my lost address book, **but** I could not find it, **so** I decided to start a new one; I knew it would be useful.

Subordinate Clauses

A **subordinate clause**, or **dependent clause**, also contains a subject and verb, but it cannot stand alone as a simple sentence. It depends on another clause in the sentence to help it do its job. Subordinate clauses look like independent clauses, but they can begin with subordinating conjunctions.

Examples:
before I knew it
so I don't forget it
whenever you're in town

SUBORDINATING CONJUNCTIONS				
after	although	as if	as long as	as much as
because	before	even if	even though	if
in order that	now that	only if	since	so
so long as	though	unless	until	when
whenever	whereas	whether	while	where

Subordinate clauses can also begin with relative pronouns.

Examples:
whom I saw earlier
whose name I forget
whichever comes first

RELATIVE PRONOUNS			
that	which	whichever	who
whoever	whose	whom	whomever

When attaching a subordinate clause to the front of a main, or independent, clause, it is necessary to use a comma between the two clauses.

Example:
Before I knew it, I was being lambasted by the angry sergeant for my comment.

When attaching a clause to the end of a main clause, no comma is needed.

Example:
Put your name and number on the card **so I don't forget it**.

Practice
Determine whether the group of words is an independent or a subordinate clause.

1. Did you know

2. He made it

3. According to Artie

4. Remember your training

5. If you go to Paris after all

6. He said he'd had enough

7. Starting with Jamie

8. Henry's excellent performance

9. I appreciate the gesture

10. Because he liked pickles

Subordinate clauses can function as three different parts of speech: a *noun*, an *adjective*, or an *adverb*.

Noun Clauses

We know that nouns can play many roles. They can be subjects, predicate nominatives, direct objects, appositives, indirect objects, or objects of prepositions. Some words that begin noun clauses are question-starters like *who, what, where, when, why, how,* as well as the words *that, whether, whom, whoever,* and *whomever.*

Example:
I see Robin.

Here, the proper noun *Robin* is the direct object of *see.*

Example:
I see that Robin finished three books already.

The noun clause *that Robin finished three books already* functions as the direct object of the verb *see.*

Example:
Charles, a local hero, received an award.

The phrase *a local hero* is an appositive phrase that modifies the noun *Charles.*

Example:
Charles, who is a local hero, received an award.

The clause *who is a local hero* is a noun clause functioning as an appositive.

Adjective and Adverb Clauses

Subordinate clauses function as adjectives when they describe or modify nouns or pronouns. Like adjectives, they answer the questions *what kind?* and *which one?* about the words they modify. An **adjective clause** begins with a word like the relative pronouns *who, whose, whom, that,* or *which,* or the subordinating conjunctions *where* or *when.*

Example:
The painting, which had a price tag of $10,000, was too expensive.

The adjective clause *which had a price tag of $10,000* is modifying the noun *painting.*

Example:
The man who witnessed the robbery was later interviewed by the newspaper.

The adjective clause *who witnessed the robbery* modifies the noun *man.*

When a subordinate clause answers *where, when, how,* or *why,* it is functioning as an adverb and is called an **adverb clause**. Like other adverbs, the adverb clause answers *where? when? why?* and *how?* about the verb, adjective, or other adverb it modifies. Adverb clauses begin with subordinating conjunctions such as *because, although, once, until,* and *after,* to name a few.

Example:
As he set the cup down, coffee spilled all over his shoe.

The adverb clause *as he set the cup down* modifies the verb *spilled.*

Example:
Allison stayed longer than David did.

The adverb clause *than David did* modifies the adverb *longer.*

Answers

1. subordinate clause
2. independent clause
3. subordinate clause
4. independent clause
5. subordinate clause
6. independent clause
7. subordinate clause
8. subordinate clause
9. independent clause
10. subordinate clause

10 Conjunctions

LESSON SUMMARY

When you write, does it matter if your connectors are correlative, coordinating, or subordinating? Does it matter if the elements being connected are similar? Find out here.

Conjunctions are connecting words. They join words, phrases, and sentences in writing and speech. Conjunctions come in three forms: *coordinating*, *correlative*, and *subordinating*. Coordinating and correlative conjunctions connect similar elements: nouns with nouns, phrases with phrases, sentences with sentences. Subordinating conjunctions connect elements that are dissimilar.

Coordinating Conjunctions

The acronym FANBOYS will help you remember the seven, and *only* seven, **coordinating conjunctions**: *for*, *and*, *nor*, *but*, *or*, *yet*, and *so*. They connect similar elements: a noun with another noun, a phrase with another phrase, an independent clause with another independent clause. (*For* and *so* can only be used to connect clauses, however.)

> **⤳ TIP**
>
> Some people think it is wrong to start a sentence with a conjunction like *and*, *but*, or *so*. Today, however, most grammar experts consider that to be perfectly acceptable. Starting a sentence with *and*, *but*, or *so* can give your writing more impact. Just don't overdo it.

COORDINATING CONJUNCTIONS

for	expresses a logical relationship, where one element is the cause of another Alice sold her condominium, for she wanted a house.
and	joins elements that are equal in importance June vacuumed the floors and dusted the furniture.
nor	presents an alternate idea or thought He doesn't have any patience for tardiness, nor will he tolerate late payments.
but	indicates a difference or exception between elements Their vacation was short but enjoyable.
or	presents an alternative or option for an element of equal importance You can have juice or soda with your meal.
yet	joins elements that follow logically but are opposing She is so glamorous yet down to earth.
so	suggests the consequence of related ideas Marge cut the grass yesterday, so she got to relax today.

> ↩ **TIP**
>
> When using a coordinating conjunction to connect two independent clauses, always place a comma directly in front of the coordinating conjunction.

Practice

In each of the following sentences, identify the coordinating conjunction and the words, phrases, or clauses it connects.

11. I thought the manuscript was sophisticated yet easy to follow.

12. Kelly or Roger is responsible for cleaning up after the store closes.

13. This tea is supposed to help relieve cold symptoms, but I haven't noticed a difference.

14. She's not sure if she wants to go to the University of Connecticut or Wesleyan University.

15. We don't expect the parent company to make a profit this quarter, nor do we foresee a turnaround for its subsidiaries.

16. Tim had to place a new order, for we were out of printer paper and toner.

17. Andrew has already agreed to paint the scenery, so I will need you or Maureen to organize the props.

18. I knew it was supposed to rain, yet I neglected to bring my umbrella.

19. The meeting starts at 8, so he is picking us up at 7:30.

20. Her New Year's resolution is to lose weight, and she has already joined a gym to get started.

Correlative Conjunctions

Correlative conjunctions come in pairs and are used as such. They connect sentence elements of similar structure and importance. There are five common pairs of correlative conjunctions.

CORRELATIVE CONJUNCTIONS	
both . . . and	Both Kelly and Ingrid attended the cooking demonstration.
either . . . or	Either you let him go or I'm calling the police.
neither . . . nor	I can neither go shopping nor go to the movies because the mall is closed.
not only . . . but also	We spent not only the summer but also the fall in Alaska.
whether . . . or	Sometimes I don't know whether Lynn or Jill should take the lead.

Practice
Insert the correlative conjunctions that make the most sense in the following sentences.

21. The IT department said our team can have _____ new computers _____ new printers because there isn't budget for both.

22. I emailed the earnings report to _____ Tammy _____ Charles, but Charles claims he never received it.

23. _____ Henry _____ Veronica wants to go to St. Louis; they'd rather go to Chicago.

24. It's unclear _____ Julie is in charge _____ Kerry is.

25. He _____ spearheaded research and development _____ oversaw production.

26. _____ does Dionne have the highest grade in the class, _____ she also completed the extra credit assignment.

27. _____ you are prepared _____ not, the presentation is on Wednesday morning.

28. _____ you want to go _____ you don't.

> **⇨ TIP**
>
> You may have noticed that *whether* is often used without its partner, *or*, for example, in the sentence "I'm not sure *whether* I can go with you." In these cases the other half of the pair is implied: "I'm not sure *whether* [*or not*] I can go with you."

Subordinating Conjunctions

Subordinating conjunctions connect an independent clause to a dependent, or subordinate, clause. (For a review of clauses, see Lesson 9.)

The table below shows some commonly used subordinating conjunctions and the type of relationship they convey. The logic of their use lies in the relationship between the two clauses at hand. For example, consider this sentence:

> The program will have to be discontinued unless more interest is generated.

The clause *unless more interest is generated* cannot stand alone because its meaning depends on the independent clause *The program will have to be discontinued.*

SUBORDINATING CONJUNCTIONS			
TIME	**CAUSE/EFFECT**	**CONDITION**	**CONTRAST**
after	because	as long as	although
before	so	unless	even though
when	now that	provided that	though
since	in order that	so long as	as much as
until	as if	if	while
as soon as		whether	whereas
whenever			even if

⤳ TIP

Think you're seeing things? You're not; many subordinating conjunctions were also listed as prepositions in Lesson 6. Don't forget—words can play many different roles in a sentence! For example, depending on its function, the word *since* can play three roles.

It can be an adverb:

> He transferred to the Philadelphia office in 2008 and has been there ever *since*.

or a preposition:

> I haven't had fresh pineapple *since* my trip to Hawaii.

or a conjunction:

> *Since* it's Mary's project, she led the presentation.

Practice

For each pair of sentences below, find a subordinating conjunction that makes sense and use it to combine them into a single sentence.

29. The *Twilight* books continue to sell well. We should publish more vampire books.

30. The pie was a little burned. It still tasted good.

31. We can't make it out to Colorado for the conference. We plan to call in for the board meeting.

32. You don't have anything to do. You can start going through the books in that box.

33. It is raining today. You should bring an umbrella along.

34. The contract is not yet signed. I have reminded Jerry.

35. We should arrive at the airport on time. We left a little late.

36. You will be eligible for a promotion. You complete your MBA.

Answers

11. sophisticated **yet** easy to follow

12. Kelly **or** Roger

13. This tea is supposed to help relieve cold symptoms, **but** I haven't noticed a difference.

14. University of Connecticut **or** Wesleyan University

15. We don't expect the parent company to make a profit this quarter, **nor** do we foresee a turnaround for its subsidiaries.

16. Tim had to place a new order, **for** we were out of printer paper and toner.

17. Andrew has already agreed to paint the scenery, **so** I will need you or Maureen to organize the props.

18. I knew it was supposed to rain, **yet** I neglected to bring my umbrella.

19. The meeting starts at 8, **so** he is picking us up at 7:30.

20. Her New Year's resolution is to lose weight, **and** she has already joined a gym to get started.

21. either . . . or

22. both . . . and

23. Neither . . . nor

24. whether . . . or

25. not only . . . but also

26. Not only . . . but

27. Whether . . . or

28. Either . . . or

29. *Because* the *Twilight* books continue to sell well, we should publish more vampire books.
So long as the *Twilight* books continue to sell well, we should publish more vampire books.
Since the *Twilight* books continue to sell well, we should publish more vampire books.
If the *Twilight* books continue to sell well, we should publish more vampire books.

As long as the *Twilight* books continue to sell well, we should publish more vampire books.

30. *Even though* the pie was a little burned, it still tasted good.

Although the pie was a little burned, it still tasted good.

31. *Because* we can't make it out to Colorado for the conference, we plan to call in for the board meeting.

32. *If* you don't have anything to do, you can start going through the books in that box.

Now that you don't have anything to do, you can start going through the books in that box.

Since you don't have anything to do, you can start going through the books in that box.

33. It is raining today, *so* you should bring an umbrella along.

Since it is raining today, you should bring an umbrella along.

Because it is raining today, you should bring an umbrella along.

You should bring an umbrella along *since* it is raining today.

You should bring an umbrella along *because* it is raining today.

34. The contract is not yet signed *even though* I have reminded Jerry.

The contract is not yet signed, *although* I have reminded Jerry.

The contract is not yet signed, *though* I have reminded Jerry.

35. We should arrive at the airport on time *even though* we left a little late.

We should arrive at the airport on time, *although* we left a little late.

Although we left a little late, we should arrive at the airport on time.

Even though we left a little late, we should arrive at the airport on time.

36. You will be eligible for a promotion *provided that* you complete your MBA.

You will be eligible for a promotion *as long as* you complete your MBA.

You will be eligible for a promotion *so long as* you complete your MBA.

You will be eligible for a promotion *before* you complete your MBA.

You will be eligible for a promotion *when* you complete your MBA.

You will be eligible for a promotion *after* you complete your MBA.

You will be eligible for a promotion *as soon as* you complete your MBA.

You will be eligible for a promotion *if* you complete your MBA.

You will be eligible for a promotion *whenever* you complete your MBA.

Provided that you complete your MBA, you will be eligible for a promotion.

As long as you complete your MBA, you will be eligible for a promotion.

So long as you complete your MBA, you will be eligible for a promotion.

Combining Sentences

LESSON SUMMARY

Good writing involves sentences of varying lengths and complexities that make text more appealing and inviting to readers. To start with, you can achieve this by combining your sentences. In this lesson, you will learn how to do just that.

f you have ever read a book written for young readers, you probably noticed that the sentences were simple, direct, and short. While that kind of language may be helpful for beginning readers, it becomes extremely monotonous and uninteresting for advanced readers. Books that are more interesting to read contain a variety of sentence lengths and complexities. Authors accomplish this by combining sentences.

Similarly, your everyday writing can benefit from varying your sentences. Have you ever had an e-mail or a letter from someone who writes nothing but long, complicated, formal sentences? If so, you may have had a difficult time trying to figure out the most important information the writer was trying to tell you. On the other side, if you're reading text made up of nothing but short, choppy sentences, you might feel like the writer is rushing and possibly missing key information. Finding a balance between the two extremes is key. Make sure the important information is easy to spot, but also make sure that you're offering enough supporting information and clauses to give your reader a complete picture of what you're saying/asking/explaining. Now that you've got the building blocks for sentences, it's time to explore how to put them together most effectively.

Besides simple sentences, there are three other kinds of basic sentences: compound, complex, and compound-complex.

We know that independent clauses are **simple sentences**, which must have, minimally, a simple subject and predicate. (See Lesson 8.)

Examples:
Nathan talks.
Les listens.
Nora laughs.

The following table maps out simple-sentence structures. These examples do not include the infinite number of modifying words, phrases, and clauses that could be added for detail.

SIMPLE-SENTENCE STRUCTURES

(Implied subject *you*) + (**V**)erb = simple sentence	*Watch!*
(**S**)ubject + **V** = simple sentence	*Sam watched.*
S + **V** + (**O**)bject =	*Sam watched baseball.*
(**C**)ompound **S** + **V** + **O** =	*Sam and Joe watched baseball.*
S + **CV** + **O** =	*Sam watched and played baseball.*
S + **V** + **CO** =	*Sam watched baseball and football.*
CS + **CV** + **O** =	*Sam and Joe watched and played baseball.*
CS + **V** + **CO** =	*Sam and Joe watched baseball and football.*
S + **CV** + **CO** =	*Sam watched and played baseball and football.*
CS + **CV** + **CO** =	*Sam and Joe watched and played baseball and football.*

Compound Sentences

Shorter sentences can be combined into one complete thought or sentence.

Example:
Nathan, Les, and Nora enjoy talking, listening, and laughing.

While that livens up the writing a bit, it is still rather limited. For more complex sentence structure, take two or more related sentences, or independent clauses, and join them with a coordinating conjunction (*for*, *and*, *nor*, *but*, *or*, *yet*, or *so*) or a semicolon to create a **compound sentence**.

Examples:
Nathan and Nora talk and laugh; Les listens.
Les listens; Nathan and Nora talk and laugh.
Nathan and Nora talk and laugh, **but** Les listens.
Les listens, **yet** Nathan and Nora talk and laugh.
Nathan and Nora talk and laugh, **so** Les listens.
Les listens, **and** Nathan and Nora talk and laugh.

The combinations are, of course, interchangeable. The coordinating conjunction *or* is a good choice if the equal subjects have an alternative. The coordinating conjunction *nor* is a better choice if the expressions are negative. The conjunction *for*, denoting "because," would work grammatically, but isn't very logical in this case.

Practice
Combine the following simple sentences to create a compound sentence.

1. My bag was already packed. I realized I should pack extra socks as well.

2. I decided to visit London for the trade show. I renewed my passport in anticipation.

3. My performance was very good this year. I sold 26% more than my sales goal.

4. The grocery store on Sandy Street was out of avocados. I found some at the farmer's market in Dempsey Park.

5. The power went out. We had no idea how long the outage would last.

6. Mark went to the concert Saturday night. Felix went too.

7. Harry has been late every day this week. He should be reprimanded.

8. Jill bought her mom a book for her birthday. Melissa bought her flowers. Brian bought her a gift card for her favorite restaurant.

9. The comedy show was hilarious. I plan to bring my friends with me to the next one.

10. We wanted to celebrate our company's anniversary. We went out to dinner.

11. It rained so much. The subways are closed due to flooding.

12. I caught a ride with my neighbor. My car wouldn't start.

13. Kyle presented his conclusions. The committee decided not to move ahead with this project.

14. Luke mowed the lawn. He earned ten dollars.

15. I stayed up late last night. I am tired today.

Complex Sentences

In addition to compound sentences, we can create **complex sentences** by combining one independent clause and one or more subordinate (dependent) clauses.

Examples:

Les sat and listened *while Nathan and Nora laughed and talked.*

While Nathan and Nora laughed and talked, Les sat and listened.

Les sat and listened *while Nathan and Nora laughed and talked, although he wasn't feeling well.*

Although he wasn't feeling well, Les sat and listened *while Nathan and Nora laughed and talked.*

⤷ TIP

Remember to put your key message in the main subject/verb position of your sentence. Do not hide it in other clauses.

Compound-Complex Sentences

Finally, we can create **compound-complex sentences**, using at least two independent clauses and one or more subordinate clauses.

Examples:

Les sat and listened *while Nathan and Nora laughed and talked,* **for** he wasn't feeling well.

While Nathan and Nora laughed and talked, Les sat and listened, **for** he wasn't feeling well.

Les wasn't feeling well, **so** he sat and listened *while Nathan and Nora laughed and talked.*

Note that the boldfaced word in each of these sentences is a conjunction.

Practice

Combine the independent and subordinate clauses to create complex or compound-complex sentences.

16. If you want to go with me to the library. You will need to be ready to leave in about ten minutes.

17. Sandra had nowhere else to be until 7:00. She ran errands around town and was able to fit in a yoga class.

18. Although the meteorologist predicted that the storm would miss us, we put out the snow shovels anyway, and Jerry salted the sidewalk in front of our house just in case.

19. Because she was confident, Liz thought she could do it on her own, but she was grateful when Myles offered to help.

20. Fred spent the afternoon cleaning out the garage, and he was pleased to find his old vinyl record collection, which he thought had been thrown out years ago.

21. I enjoyed the book, but I didn't care for the movie, which changed everything except the characters' names.

22. When he volunteered at the senior center, Kevin made a lot of friends, and he learned to love playing Scrabble.

23. If you want to lower your cholesterol, doctors advise exercising more and eating better.

24. The watercress salad was disappointing, but the chicken entrée was fantastic, with its crisp skin and fresh herbs.

25. After I hit the snooze button about six times, it was inevitable that I would be late to work.

Appositive Phrases

By adding modifiers in the form of adjectives, adverbs, or phrases to any type of sentence, we can make it even more interesting:

> Nathan and Nora, **best friends**, talked and laughed **about last night's party**, but Les, **who wasn't feeling well**, just sat **quietly** and listened.

The appositive phrase *best friends*, the adverb phrase *about last night's party*, the noun clause *who wasn't feeling well*, and the adverb *quietly* were added to the sentences to provide more information about the subjects *Nathan*, *Nora*, and *Les* and the predicates *laughed*, *talked*, and *sat*. Vivid details such as these make sentences more attention grabbing and inviting to read.

⮑ TIP

When you write, read your more complex sentences aloud and then make changes until you find the smoothest, most effective combinations.

Answers

(Possible answers are shown.)

1. My bag was already packed, **but** I realized I should pack extra socks as well.

2. I decided to visit London for the trade show, **so** I renewed my passport in anticipation.

3. My performance was very good this year, **as** I sold 26% more than my sales goal.

4. The grocery store on Sandy Street was out of avocados, **but** I found some at the farmer's market in Dempsey Park.

5. The power went out, **and** we had no idea how long the outage would last.

6. Mark went to the concert on Saturday night, **and** Felix went too.

7. **Because** Harry has been late every day this week, he should be reprimanded.

8. Jill bought her mom a book for her birthday, Melissa bought her flowers, **and** Brian bought her a gift card for her favorite restaurant.

9. The comedy show was hilarious, **so** I plan to bring my friends with me to the next one.

10. We went out to dinner, **for** we wanted to celebrate our company's anniversary.

11. It rained so much **that** the subways were closed due to flooding.

12. I caught a ride with my neighbor **as** my car wouldn't start.

13. **After** Kyle presented his conclusions, the committee decided not to move ahead with this project.

14. Luke mowed the lawn, **and** he earned ten dollars.

15. I stayed up late last night, **so** I am tired today.

16. If you want to go with me to the library, you will need to be ready to leave in about ten minutes. (complex)

17. Because Sandra had nowhere else to be until 7:00, she ran errands around town and was able to fit in a yoga class. (complex)

18. Although the meteorologist predicted that the storm would miss us, we put out the snow shovels anyway, and Jerry salted the sidewalk in front of our house just in case. (compound-complex)

19. Because she was confident, Liz thought she could do it on her own, but she was grateful when Myles offered to help. (compound-complex)

20. Fred spent the afternoon cleaning out the garage, and he was pleased to find his old vinyl record collection, which he thought had been thrown out years ago. (compound-complex)

21. I enjoyed the book, but I didn't care for the movie, which changed everything except the characters' names. (compound-complex)

22. When he volunteered at the senior center, Kevin made a lot of friends, and he learned to love playing Scrabble. (compound-complex)

23. If you want to lower your cholesterol, doctors advise exercising more and eating better. (complex)

24. The watercress salad was disappointing, but the chicken entrée was fantastic, with its crisp skin and fresh herbs. (compound)

25. After I hit the snooze button about six times, it was inevitable that I would be late to work. (complex)

Section 5: Punctuation

Cut out all those exclamation marks. An exclamation mark is like laughing at your own joke.

—F. Scott Fitzgerald, American author

We've all seen sloppy punctuation in everyday writing, inside the workplace and out of it. *Is that sentence missing a period because the writer forgot it, or has the last half of the sentence been chopped off? Without any commas in this sentence, how am I supposed to tell what the writer is asking me to do?*

Because punctuation is often our road map in a block of text, giving a quick glimpse at the structure, it affects the flow of what we read. When the punctuation is missing or incorrect, it's often obvious to the reader—which can distract from the point you are trying to make. Say you're presenting slides in front of a number of people . . . would you want people in the room to focus on the extra commas onscreen, or do you want them to pay attention to your great bullet points? Taking care with punctuation will smooth out your writing—think of it as the finishing touch.

12 End Punctuation

LESSON SUMMARY
Review the basics of end punctuation and its proper placement in sentences and abbreviations.

Periods

The most common form of end punctuation, the **period** (.) indicates the end of declarative sentences (statements of facts) and imperative sentences (simple commands or requests).

Examples:
The team earned a pizza party this month.
Order an extra-large pepperoni pizza with mushrooms,
    please.

Periods are also used with common abbreviations, such as months, days, and measurements (Dec., Mon., in.). Note that periods are *not* used for acronyms—abbreviations that use all capital letters (NATO, CEO, DNA)—or for postal state abbreviations (SD, AL,

NJ). Finally, periods are used in a person's initials (T. S. Eliot, W. C. Fields) and in titles such as Dr., Mr., and Gov. If a sentence ends with an abbreviation that has an end period, use it as the end mark, unless the sentence needs an exclamation point or question mark.

Example:
It happened at exactly 3 P.M.

But:
It happened at exactly 3 P.M.!
Did it happen at exactly 3 P.M.?

Periods Checklist

Use periods in the following cases:

- At the end of a declarative sentence (sentence that makes a statement)→*Today, I took a walk to nowhere.*
- At the end of a command or request→*Here's a cloth. Now gently burp the baby on your shoulder.*
- At the end of an indirect question→*Jane asked if I knew where she had left her keys.*
- Before a decimal number→*Statisticians say that the average family raises 2.5 children.*
- Between dollars and cents→*I remember when $1.50 could buy the coolest stuff.*
- After an initial in a person's name→*You are Sir James W. Dewault, are you not?*
- After an abbreviation→*On Jan. 12, I leave for Africa.*

Practice

Add periods where they belong in the sentences below.

1. Dr Martin Luther King, Jr was born on Jan 15, 1929, but the holiday celebrating his birth is always on the third Monday of the month, even if it's not the 15th

2. I had a 20 dollar bill and a dime, so I was just barely able to purchase a ticket for the 7:35 PM train to Albany, which cost $2005

3. The great showman P T Barnum once said, "There's a sucker born every minute"

4. On a school trip to Washington, DC, my class and I got to meet former president George H W Bush and former surgeon general M Joycelyn Elders, MD

5. After she graduated from law school, she was able to add "JD" and "Esq" to her name on official documents

Question Marks

The **question mark** (?) indicates the end of an interrogatory sentence (direct question).

Examples:
Isn't this difficult?
May I try this time?
Are you okay?

Indirect questions are statements that only sound like questions, so they end with a period.

Example:
She saw the frustrated look on my face and asked if she could help me. I asked her where the laundry detergent was.

Question Marks Checklist

Use question marks in the following cases:

- At the end of a question → *Why do you look so sad?*
- Inside a quotation mark when the quotation is a question → *She asked, "Why do you look so sad?"*

Exclamation Points

An **exclamation point** (!) at the end of a sentence indicates strong feelings or authoritative commands. Interjections—free-standing words or phrases that express strong feelings—are also punctuated with exclamation points.

> **Examples:**
> Wow! What a great idea!
> Look where you're going!

⇨ TIP

Using two or more exclamation points at the end of a sentence for extra emphasis may seem like a good idea, but in fact it is incorrect and may be thought of as rude.

Exclamation Points Checklist

Use exclamation points in the following cases:

- At the end of a word, phrase, or sentence filled with emotion → *Hurry up! I cannot be late for the meeting!*
- Inside a quotation mark when the quotation is an exclamation → *The woman yelled, "Hurry up! I cannot be late for the meeting!"*

Practice

Add periods, question marks, and exclamation points where they belong in the sentences below.

6. "Congratulations" Sam exclaimed, before nosily asking us how much the wedding cost

7. "Can you let me know where to find Dr Simmons's office" Michael asked

8. Did you know that David O. Russell has a new movie coming out next week

9. "The ratings for the morning show *How Are You, San Francisco* are through the roof" he exclaimed

10. Help I am going to drop all of these files

Answers

1. Dr. Martin Luther King, Jr. was born on Jan. 15, 1929, but the holiday celebrating his birth is always on the third Monday of the month, even if it's not the 15th.

2. I had a 20 dollar bill and a dime, so I was just barely able to purchase a ticket for the 7:35 P.M. train to Albany, which cost $20.05.

3. The great showman P. T. Barnum once said, "There's a sucker born every minute."

4. On a school trip to Washington, D.C., my class and I got to meet former president George H. W. Bush and former surgeon general M. Joycelyn Elders, M.D.

5. After she graduated from law school, she was able to add "J.D." and "Esq." to her name on official documents.

6. "Congratulations!" Sam exclaimed, before nosily asking us how much the wedding cost.

7. "Can you let me know where to find Dr. Simmons's office?" Michael asked.

8. Did you know that David O. Russell has a new movie coming out next week?

9. "The ratings for the morning show *How Are You, San Francisco?* are through the roof!" he exclaimed.

10. Help! I am going to drop all of these files!

13

Commas, Colons, and Semicolons

LESSON SUMMARY

Commas, colons, and semicolons: They are ordinary kinds of punctuation, but they can be tricky. Learn where and when it is appropriate, and necessary, to use these often misused marks.

Commas

You find **commas** everywhere. They indicate a pause in writing, just as taking a breath is a pause in speaking. Commas are used to set apart some modifiers, phrases, and clauses and to enhance clarity by adding a sense of pace in written materials. There are some hard-and-fast rules for comma placement, but usage can often be a matter of personal style. Some writers use them frequently, and others do not. Just keep this in mind as you write: too many or too few commas can obscure the meaning of your message.

In a business setting, it's essential that you use commas correctly. Whether you're writing a report or an e-mail, it can be very frustrating for a reader to have to decode several lines of text that have too few comma breaks. After all, you'd pause for breath if you were speaking, right?

It can also be distracting if you use too many commas and clauses in a single sentence. Long, complicated sentences can be confusing. And during a busy day, you and your colleagues want the most important information in the easiest format. Therefore, you want your information to be as straightforward as possible. You can do this by knowing when to use commas and when to break up your content into multiple sentences.

On the following pages, you'll find some basic rules about comma use.

Rule 1. Use commas to separate a series of three or more words, phrases, or clauses in a sentence.

> **Examples:**
> Please pick up **your building ID, insurance forms, and parking pass** on your first day.
> Shelly **grabbed her coat, put it on,** and **ran to the bus**.

However, if your series uses the words *and* or *or* to connect the elements, then a comma is not necessary.

> **Examples:**
> Red **and** white **and** blue are patriotic colors.
> I cannot look at pictures of snakes **or** spiders **or** mice without anxiety.
>
> **Not:**
> Red**, and** white**, and** blue are patriotic colors.
> I cannot look at pictures of snakes**, or** spiders**, or** mice without anxiety.

If you use two or more adjectives to describe a noun or pronoun, use a comma to separate them.

Example:
He was a **happy, intelligent** child.

Be careful not to put a comma between the final adjective and the word it modifies.

Rule 2. Set off an introductory word or phrase from the rest of the sentence with a comma. (See Lesson 13 for a review of phrases.)
This pause stops readers from carrying the meaning of the introduction into the main part of the sentence, which might lead to misinterpretation.

Confusing:
After eating the flower shop owner and his manager tallied the day's receipts.

It seems as though someone was very hungry. . . .

Less Confusing:
After eating, the flower shop owner and his manager tallied the day's receipts.

Confusing:
Laughing Larry tried to tell the joke but just couldn't.

What a strange name, Laughing Larry. . . .

Less Confusing:
Laughing, Larry tried to tell the joke but just couldn't.

A transitional phrase should also be set off by a comma if it introduces a sentence or by two commas if it is within the sentence.

Examples:
Fluke has two eyes on its left side and is, **in fact,** known
as summer flounder.
On the other hand, winter flounder has two eyes on its
right side.

Rule 3. An appositive, a word or phrase that renames or enhances a noun, should be set off from the rest of the sentence by commas.

Examples:
You, **Nancy,** are the winner.
Our neighbor, **a well-known architect,** helped us draw
up the plans.
An experienced sailor, Marie was unconcerned about
the high waves.

These appositive phrases set off by commas are nonrestrictive, or not essential; even if they are removed, the sentence will remain complete.

Rule 4. Use commas in dates, addresses, and non-business-letter salutations and closings.

Dates
Use commas after the day of the week, the day of the month, and the year (only if the sentence continues):

Our Cirque du Soleil tickets are for Wednesday, July 18, at
Madison Square Garden in New York, NY.

⤳ TIP

If you are writing only the day and month or the month and year in a sentence, do not include a comma.

Examples:
The Cirque du Soleil show was on July 18.
The last time I saw a circus was in June 2007.

Addresses

When writing an address on an envelope or at the head of a letter, use a comma only before an apartment number or state abbreviation.

Example:
Marshall Grates
122 Ridge Road, Apt. 10
Ulysses Junction, MN 57231

When referring to an address within a sentence, use additional commas to substitute for line breaks.

Example:
Please send the order to Marshall Grates, 122 Ridge Road, Apt. 10, Ulysses Junction, MN 57231.

Notice that no commas are necessary between the state and the ZIP code. However, when alluding to a city and state in a sentence (without the ZIP code), use a comma after the state.

Example:
I traveled through St. Louis, MO, on my way to Chicago.

The same rule applies for a city and country.

Example:
Sometimes Elaine travels to Paris, France, in the fall.

Salutations and Closings

When writing a letter, use a comma after the person's name and after your closing. Note that a business letter salutation requires a colon rather than a comma.

	PERSONAL LETTER	BUSINESS LETTER
Salutation	Dear Mrs. Ramirez,	Dear Sir/Madam:
Closing	Love,	Sincerely,
	Yours truly,	Respectfully,
	Fondly,	Best regards,

Rule 5. Use commas before the coordinating conjunctions *for, and, nor, but, or, yet,* and *so* if they are followed by an independent clause.

Examples:
Frank is retired, **and** his wife, Louise, will retire this year.
Frank is retired, **yet** his wife, Louise, will work for another three years.

Rule 6. Use commas before, within, and after direct quotations (the exact words someone says), whether the speaker is identified at the beginning or the end.

Examples:
Drew said, "Our trip to Aruba was awesome."
"Our trip to Aruba," Drew said, "was awesome."
"Our trip to Aruba was awesome," Drew said.

Note that an indirect quote means someone is conveying what someone else said. Do not use commas to set off the speaker in an indirect quotation.

Example:
Drew said that their trip to Aruba was awesome.

Rule 7. Commas are used with titles and degrees only when they follow the person's name.

Examples:
Arthur Mari, M.D.
Sandy Dugan, Ph.D.
Dr. Foster
Dr. Sandy Dugan

Rule 8. Commas are used in numbers longer than three digits.

In order to make a long number like 1479363072 easier to read, it is customary to place commas by grouping numbers into threes from *right to left*, dividing them into thousands, ten thousands, hundred thousands, and so on: 1,479,363,072.

Exceptions to this rule are phone numbers, page numbers, ZIP codes, years, serial numbers, and house numbers.

Example:
Edison, NJ, has five ZIP codes: 08817, 08818, 08820, 08837, and 08899.

As in any other series, commas should be placed between whole numbers in a series of numbers.

Example:
Refer to pages 466, 467, and 468 in the phone book to find information on ZIP codes.

Practice

Add commas where necessary in the following sentences or phrases.

1. Please make sure the next office supply order includes blue pens binder clips notebooks and dry-erase markers.

2. Because the vice president has laryngitis she will be unable to give the keynote speech on Tuesday March 15.

3. "Oh I didn't know you were here" she said "or I wouldn't have played the music so loud."

4. Houston Texas is the site of the annual Chili Festival where they feature amateur cooks local restaurants and great chili recipes from all over the country.

5. Either I'm going crazy or some kind of animal is making noise in the attic.

6. She had to buy the dog a new bed for he had chewed up his old one.

7. The nurse disinfected the cut on my hand put a bandage on it and told me to be more careful when slicing bagels.

8. When I ran into my favorite celebrity on the street in New York she graciously agreed to have a picture taken with me Aunt Sally and my dad.

9. For our anniversary in September which will be our third we will be vacationing in Acapulco Mexico.

10. The twins actually have different birthdays because Nicholas was born at 11:58 P.M. on Monday June 3 and Nathan was born at 12:02 A.M. on Tuesday June 4.

Colons

Colons are used to introduce a word, sentence, list, quotation, or phrase. They say *here is an example* or *an example is going to follow*.

Example:
On your first day of the art workshop, please bring the following items to room 601 of Larsson Hall: a charcoal pencil, two paintbrushes, a drawing pad, and your creativity.

Do not use a colon when introducing a list if the colon follows a preposition or a verb.

Incorrect:
On your first day of the art workshop, please bring: a charcoal pencil, two paintbrushes, a drawing pad, and your creativity to room 601 of Larsson Hall.

A colon can also introduce an excerpt or long quotation in your writing.

Example:
Benjamin Franklin (1706–1790), diplomat, politician, physicist, writer, and inventor, is quoted as saying: "All human situations have their inconveniences. We feel those of the present but neither see nor feel those of the future; and hence we often make troublesome changes without amendment, and frequently for the worse."

A colon can set off the subtitle of a movie or book.

Examples:
Phenomenal Women: Four Poems Celebrating Women is written by Maya Angelou, one of America's finest female poets.
The success of the book *The Hunger Games: Mockingjay* inspired a movie adaptation as well.

Colons are used to separate the hour from minutes in written time.

The next open appointment is at 10:20 A.M.

Semicolons

Also called the "super comma," the **semicolon** is used to link two topic-related independent clauses (sentences) when a coordinating conjunction is not used.

Examples:
Steven's sister, Haley, is short. Steven is tall.
Steven's sister, Haley, is short; Steven is tall.

Do not join two independent clauses with a comma instead of a semicolon, as doing so would create what is called a comma splice.

Use a semicolon between two independent clauses joined by a coordinating conjunction (*for, and, nor, but, or, yet,* or *so*) only when commas are also used in the sentence.

Example:
Because Haley is 6'2" tall, she is taller than most people; *but* she is the shortest sibling in her family.

 TIP

Remember, whatever follows a semicolon has to be able to stand on its own as a complete sentence.

Use a semicolon between two independent clauses separated by a transitional word or phrase or by a conjunctive adverb.

Example:
At 6'8", Steven is tall; *therefore,* even at 6'2", Steven's sister, Haley, is short in her family.

COMMON CONJUNCTIVE ADVERBS		
afterward	accordingly	besides
coincidentally	consequently	furthermore
hence	however	indeed
instead	likewise	moreover
nevertheless	nonetheless	otherwise
similarly	so	still
then	therefore	thus

Practice

Add colons and semicolons where necessary in the following sentences.

11. On his to-do list, he had the following items rake the yard, call the plumber, pick up Chinese takeout for dinner, and call Francine.

12. His new book, *The CEO Secret Finding Your Inner Executive*, is available for sale now if you go to the bookstore on Saturday, he'll be signing copies.

13. The Tampa Bay Rays have lost six games in a row however, I believe they can still turn things around and make the playoffs.

14. The book had the following dedication "To Rosemary I couldn't have done this without you."

15. After the scandal broke, the disgraced celebrity made a statement to the press "No comment."

16. Peggy knew she would have to tell the truth to Pete eventually she hoped he'd forget about the topic in the meantime, though.

17. After counting all of my money, I discovered that I had $1,453 in my savings account $756 in my checking account and $43 in my change jar, which I keep on my dresser.

18. At 400, Roger realized that Chantelle probably wasn't coming he waited for ten more minutes just in case, then went home.

COMMAS, COLONS, AND SEMICOLONS

19. Jamie wants to borrow these DVDs from you *Gray's Anatomy*, Seasons 1 and 2 *Breaking Bad*, Season 3 and *The Vampire Diaries*, Season 1.

20. Our power went out during the hurricane three days later, we're still waiting for the power company to fix it.

Answers

1. Please make sure the next office supply order includes blue pens, binder clips, notebooks, and dry-erase markers.

2. Because the vice president has laryngitis, she will be unable to give the keynote speech on Tuesday, March 15.

3. "Oh, I didn't know you were here," she said, "or I wouldn't have played the music so loud."

4. Houston, Texas, is the site of the annual Chili Festival, where they feature amateur cooks, local restaurants, and great chili recipes from all over the country.

5. Either I'm going crazy or some kind of animal is making noise in the attic.

6. She had to buy the dog a new bed, for he had chewed up his old one.

7. The nurse disinfected the cut on my hand, put a bandage on it, and told me to be more careful when slicing bagels.

8. When I ran into my favorite celebrity on the street in New York, she graciously agreed to have a picture taken with me, Aunt Sally, and my dad.

9. For our anniversary in September, which will be our third, we will be vacationing in Acapulco, Mexico.

10. The twins actually have different birthdays because Nicholas was born at 11:58 P.M. on Monday, June 3, and Nathan was born at 12:02 A.M. on Tuesday, June 4.

11. On his to-do list, he had the following items: rake the yard, call the plumber, pick up Chinese takeout for dinner, and call Francine.

12. His new book, *The CEO Secret: Finding Your Inner Executive*, is available for sale now; if you go to the bookstore on Saturday, he'll be signing copies.

13. The Tampa Bay Rays have lost six games in a row; however, I believe they can still turn things around and make the playoffs.

14. The book had the following dedication: "To Rosemary: I couldn't have done this without you."

15. After the scandal broke, the disgraced celebrity made a statement to the press: "No comment."

16. Peggy knew she would have to tell the truth to Pete eventually; she hoped he'd forget about the topic in the meantime, though.

17. After counting all of my money, I discovered that I had $1,453 in my savings account; $756 in my checking account; and $43 in my change jar, which I keep on my dresser.

18. At 4:00, Roger realized that Chantelle probably wasn't coming; he waited for ten more minutes just in case, then went home.

19. Jamie wants to borrow these DVDs from you: *Grey's Anatomy*, Seasons 1 and 2; *Breaking Bad*, Season 3; and *The Vampire Diaries*, Season 1.

20. Our power went out during the hurricane; three days later, we're still waiting for the power company to fix it.

14

Apostrophes, Hyphens, and Dashes

LESSON SUMMARY

This chapter shows you how, where, and when to use three little marks that are easy to misplace.

Apostrophes

Apostrophes are used to create contractions, to make nouns possessive, and, in rare instances, to make nouns plural.

Contractions

Contract means to squeeze together or shorten. In informal writing, we shorten two words into one, using an apostrophe to create a **contraction**. For instance, *has* and *not* become *hasn't*. The following tables show some other common contractions.

PRONOUN CONTRACTIONS			
	AM/IS/ARE	**WILL**	**HAVE/HAS**	**HAD/WOULD**
I	I'm	I'll	I've	I'd
you	you're	you'll	you've	you'd
he	he's	he'll	he's	he'd
she	she's	she'll	she's	she'd
it	it's	it'll	it's	it'd
we	we're	we'll	we've	we'd
they	they're	they'll	they've	they'd

Note that contractions are typically not used in formal writing, such as proposals, reports, and letters to clients or customers. However, there may be times where more informal writing is appropriate— like writing one-on-one e-mails to colleagues you know well. If you're ever in doubt about how formal your writing should be, it is better to be cautious and err on the side of formality in the work- place. If you are unsure, read what you've written and ask yourself whether the tone and language are something you would want your boss or your entire company to read.

NEGATIVE CONTRACTIONS			
is	+	not	=	isn't
are	+	not	=	aren't
was	+	not	=	wasn't
were	+	not	=	weren't
have	+	not	=	haven't
has	+	not	=	hasn't
had	+	not	=	hadn't
can	+	not	=	can't
do	+	not	=	don't
did	+	not	=	didn't
should	+	not	=	shouldn't
would	+	not	=	wouldn't
could	+	not	=	couldn't

Possessive Nouns

You learned a bit about possessives in Lesson 1. Let's review this tricky concept once again. **Possessives** are nouns that show ownership. To make a singular noun possessive, add -'s. Be careful not to confuse the plural form of a noun with the possessive.

Plural:
The writer of the news **stories** won a Pulitzer.

Singular Possessive:
The news **story's** writer won a Pulitzer.

The first sentence tells us that the writer of multiple stories won a Pulitzer. The second sentence tells us that the writer of one story won a Pulitzer.

To form the possessive of the plural noun *stories*, add an apostrophe at the end of the word.

Plural Possessive:
The news **stories'** writer won a Pulitzer.

This sentence also tells us that the writer of multiple stories won a Pulitzer. The -s' rule applies only to plural nouns ending with an *s*. For example, the possessive of the plural noun *children* would be *children's*.

To form the possessive of a singular noun ending with *s*, add -'s.

Example:
I finally met my **boss's** wife.

Plurals with Apostrophe + s

There are a few occasions when -'s is required to make a noun plural.

Add -'s to form the plural of abbreviations that contain more than one period, such as Ph.D. or M.D.

> **Example:**
> **M.D.'s** and **Ph.D.'s** are doctorate degrees in medicine and philosophy.

Add -'s to form the plural of words, letters, and numbers that we do not commonly see in the plural form.

> **Examples:**
> How many **um's** and **uh's** did you count in the run-through of my speech?
> My son got four **A's** and two **B's** on his report card.
> Please write your **5's** and **8's** more clearly on receipts.

Practice

Place apostrophes where they belong in the following sentences.

1. Grannys recipe for apple pie was featured in *Ladies Home Journal* in 1964.

2. Jesss bike was stolen after she forgot to lock it outside the library.

3. Paul and Joanies house has been on the market for six months now.

4. "Its a shame you couldnt make it to the Diazes party," Orville said.

5. My doctors handwriting is horrible; I cant tell the difference between her 1s and her 7s.

6. The childrens test results put them among the top scorers in the state.

7. Why dont you set that box down over there, next to Louiss suitcase?

8. I ended up borrowing Maxs laptop, his mothers tablet, and my parents scanner to use in my computer training classes.

9. Wouldnt you rather get four As and one C in your classes than get all Bs, or its not important to you?

10. Youre the expert here, so I could use your advice.

11. I havent heard from Daniel in a week.

12. Lindas best friends name is Grace.

13. It wasnt Tricias fault that Kyles keys got lost.

14. The companies policy on tardiness is strict.

15. The clients March invoice is missing.

Hyphens and Dashes

Although they look similar, **hyphens** (-) and **dashes** (—) perform completely different jobs. In general, hyphens are used to connect two words or used *within* a word. Dashes are used on a bigger scale, to connect—or separate—parts of a sentence.

Hyphens

Hyphens have many uses in the English language, but arguably their most special power is the ability to clarify your message to the reader. How?

Consider this example:

> I just became a member of Greenville Professionals, a small business association in my town.

Now, is Greenville Professionals a business association that is small? Or an association that's focused on small businesses?

Without a hyphen, you'll never know. If Greenville Professionals is an association that's focused on small businesses, you can simply add a hyphen:

> I just became a member of Greenville Professionals, a small-business association in my town.

Using a hyphen here shows that the adjective *small* describes the noun *business*, and then both of those words together describe *association*.

Here's another example:

> MJ&J, a Spanish wine importer, saw its profits increase by 20% last year.

Written this way, the sentence gives confusing information to the reader. What exactly is a Spanish wine importer? Is it a Spanish company that imports wine to Spain? Or is it a company based somewhere else—say, Texas—that specializes in importing Spanish wine?

If you want to say that MJ&J imports Spanish wine, you simply need to add a hyphen:

> MJ&J, a Spanish-wine importer, saw its profits increase by 20% last year.

If you want to say that MJ&J is an import company located in Spain, it's best to revise the descriptive phrase a bit. For example, you could say:

> MJ&J, a wine importer based in Spain, saw its profits increase by 20% last year.

Hyphens help readers group words together and detangle ideas. For example, look at this sentence:

> As a former human resources manager, I tell my clients one easy to remember rule of thumb: always negotiate with your new employer, even if you're being hired for a short term or contract based project.

Unlike the MJ&J example, the meaning of this sentence is clear even without commas. But it's not a fun sentence to read. As you read, your brain has to group different words together to see what makes sense (*former human* or *human resources*? *easy to remember rule* or *remember rule of thumb*?). By using hyphens, you can help your reader quickly understand what you're trying to communicate:

> As a former human-resources manager, I tell my clients one easy-to-remember rule of thumb: always negotiate with your new employer, even if you're being hired for a short-term or contract-based project.

As a general rule, when two or more words work together as a unit to describe a noun (or nouns) that comes after them, consider using a hyphen. While grammar experts vary in their opinion of how necessary hyphens are for readability, here are some examples of the many terms that should definitely include a hyphen:

a **snow-removal** company

an **income-tax** form

a **last-man-standing** attitude

a long, **drawn-out** process

a surprisingly affordable **business-class** ticket

a **fast-moving** process

a **custom-made** linen suit

a **once-in-a-lifetime** opportunity

a **desert-island-like** sense of community

a new **neighborhood-watch** group

an annoying **paper-cut** injury

a **20-year** contract

a **long-term, long-distance** relationship

a **world-renowned** motivational speaker

mail-in rebates and coupons

a **red-brick** townhouse

a **brick-red** dinner jacket

a **hit-or-miss** question

Another important place where hyphens can be found is within individual words, for instance to join a prefix, such as *ex-*, *pro-*, *anti-*, and *self-*, to a root word. Look at these examples:

ex-husband

ex-president

pro-union

pro-life

anti-abortion

anti-American

self-made

self-aware

Keep in mind that most words that contain a prefix *don't* use a hyphen; among the many hyphen-free examples are *antihero* (*anti- + hero*), *undone* (*un- + done*), *rewrite* (*re- + write*), and *disappear* (*dis- + appear*). So how do you know when a word is spelled with a hyphen?

The rules for using hyphens within single words are too detailed to explain and often highly inconsistent. The best solution is simply to look up the word you're wondering about in a major dictionary, such as Merriam Webster's.

One reason that they're used with prefixes is to avoid confusion. For instance, does the word *recover* mean to cover again or does it mean to bring something back? If you want to indicate that it means cover again, add a hyphen. If you want it to mean bring something back, leave it hyphen-free.

Examples:

At the upholstery shop, we can **re-cover** your sofa or chair with any fabric you choose.

If the company can **recover** even 50 percent of its losses, I'll be content.

Hyphens are also used to join words together to create other words. For example:

step-sister	part-time
father-in-law	merry-go-round
great-grandparents	editor-in-chief
jump-start	passer-by

And they're used to spell out the numbers 21 through 99 and fractions. For example:

twenty-one	three-fifths
thirty-five	one-third

When Not to Use Hyphens

As we mentioned, the rules for using hyphens can be complicated and not always agreed upon. Follow the guidelines above and use a dictionary when you are not sure. However, there four occasions when, with few exceptions, you should *not use* a hyphen:

1. **With adverbs that end in -*ly*.** When an adverb such as *quickly* or *beautifully* is used with another word to describe

a noun, you don't need to use a hyphen to connect them. For example:

Incorrect:
Our shop is known for delivering **beautifully-arranged** flowers within an hour or less.

Correct:
Our shop is known for delivering **beautifully arranged** flowers within an hour or less.

2. **When a string of descriptive words come after the noun.**
Look at how hyphens are used, and not used, in the following examples, all of which are correct:

She is a **well-regarded** <u>attorney</u>.
But:
That <u>attorney</u> is **well regarded**.
I booked a **half-hour** <u>massage</u>.
But:
The <u>massage</u> is a **half hour**.
He has a nearly **three-month-old** <u>baby</u>.
But:
His <u>baby</u> is nearly **three months old**.
Here are some **easy-to-follow** <u>instructions</u>.
But:
These <u>instructions</u> are **easy to follow**.

As we discussed, when words are used together to describe a noun, it's usually necessary or helpful to the reader to join those words with hyphens. But when the descriptive words come *after* the noun, the hyphens are not needed. Why? When you move them after the noun, you are already separating the descriptive words from the noun (with a verb, such as *is*). The words will already be grouped together in the right way, so you don't need to help the reader by adding hyphens.

3. **When a proper name describes a noun.** For example:
   Incorrect:
   Two **New-York-Times** reporters first broke the story.
   Correct:
   Two **New York Times** reporters first broke the story.
   Yes, we're using the words *New York Times* as a description of the noun reporters, and yes, it comes before the noun. However, there's no need to connect the words *New, York,* and *Times* with hyphens because they already stand together as a single unit—as the proper name of the newspaper. Here's one more example:
   Incorrect:
   He bought 10 shares of **Berkshire-Hathaway** stock.
   Correct:
   He bought 10 shares of **Berkshire Hathaway** stock.

4. **With *very.*** For example:
   Incorrect:
   It's a **very-cost-effective** plan.
   Correct:
   It's a **very cost-effective** plan.

Practice

Add hyphens as needed below.

16. I bought a one way ticket on the Acela Express.

17. Steven is filled with little known facts and other useless information.

18. As a hedge fund manager, I have a bird's eye view of the global financial markets.

19. After years of hard work and living paycheck to paycheck, he was finally promoted to senior staff.

20. Your vacation is certainly well deserved, but I wouldn't spend two thirds of your savings on it.

21. All of their close friends had huge, break the bank weddings, but Sara and Dan decided on a more intimate, family only affair.

22. It's a challenging three year training program, but when they complete it, most associates land well paying jobs within a few weeks.

23. Jada and her ex husband still work together at the real estate company they founded twenty five years ago.

24. For some strange reason, I find fill in the blank questions more difficult than essay questions.

25. Caroline has a two month old daughter, a one year old son, and a step daughter who just turned eight.

Dashes

In workplace and personal writing, the most useful type of **dash** is the long dash (or "em-dash"). It is used to help a phrase or clause stand apart from the rest of the sentence.

> **Example:**
> Louis's favorite color is—let me guess—pink!

Like a colon, but less formal, an em-dash can be used to set off a short series of phrases or words in a sentence.

> **Example:**
> My MBA program let me explore several different areas—marketing, accounting, and sales—before I chose a specialty.

Practice

Add hyphens and dashes as needed in the following sentences.

26. I'm really lucky I get along well with my mother in law and father in law.

27. The president elect delivered a thrilling election night speech.

28. This is my favorite T shirt I've worn it so much that you can barely tell what color it was originally.

29. Minnie thought the other player was bluffing, so she went all in on her poker hand.

30. It wasn't until the mid 1980s that the band became popular but since then, they've been a constant presence.

31. We won't know the test scores until tomorrow at that point, we can figure out if we need to retake the test.

32. Marcy never one to shy away from conflict confronted the man who had cut in front of her in the checkout line.

33. Shani went to the all American team's rally but left after the first few speeches.

34. His favorite historical period to study is pre Columbian America, but World War II is a close second.

35. More often than not, his devil may care attitude got him in trouble.

Answers

1. Granny's recipe for apple pie was featured in *Ladies' Home Journal* in 1964.
2. Jess's bike was stolen after she forgot to lock it outside the library.
3. Paul and Joanie's house has been on the market for six months now.
4. "It's a shame you couldn't make it to the Diazes' party," Orville said.
5. Remember, when you set out the cats' food: Mr. Snuffles gets the special food for elderly cats, and Buddy gets the regular kibble.
6. The children's test results put them among the top scorers in the state.
7. Why don't you set that box down over there, next to Louis's suitcase?
8. I borrowed Melanie's and Jason's notes, because I missed Monday's class.
9. Your entry won't count if you don't make sure it's post-marked by the contest's deadline of January 15.
10. You're the expert here, so I could use your advice.
11. I haven't heard from Daniel in a week.
12. Linda's best friend's name is Grace.
13. It wasn't Tricia's fault that Kyle's keys got lost.
14. The companies' policy on tardiness is strict.
15. The client's March invoice is missing.
16. I bought a one-way ticket on the Acela Express.
17. Steven is filled with little-known facts and other useless information.
18. As a hedge-fund manager, I have a bird's-eye view of the global financial markets.
19. After years of hard work and living paycheck to paycheck, he was finally promoted to senior staff. [*no hyphens needed*]

20. Your vacation is certainly well deserved, but I wouldn't spend two-thirds of your savings on it.

21. All of their close friends had huge, break-the-bank weddings, but Sara and Dan decided on a more intimate, family-only affair.

22. It's a challenging three-year training program, but when they complete it, most associates land well-paying jobs within a few weeks.

23. Jada and her ex-husband still work together at the real-estate company they founded twenty-five years ago.

24. For some strange reason, I find fill-in-the-blank questions more difficult than essay questions.

25. Caroline has a two-month-old daughter, a one-year-old son, and a step-daughter who just turned eight.

26. I'm really lucky—I get along well with my mother-in-law and father-in-law.

27. The president-elect delivered a thrilling election-night speech.

28. This is my favorite T-shirt—I've worn it so much that you can barely tell what color it was originally.

29. Minnie thought the other player was bluffing, so she went all-in on her poker hand.

30. It wasn't until the mid-1980s that the band became popular—but since then, they've been a constant presence.

31. We won't know the test scores until tomorrow—at that point, we can figure out if we need to retake the test.

32. Marcy—never one to shy away from conflict—confronted the man who had cut in front of her in the checkout line.

33. Shani went to the all-American team's rally but left after the first few speeches.

34. His favorite historical period to study is pre-Columbian America, but World War II is a close second.

35. More often than not, his devil-may-care attitude got him in trouble.

15

Quotation Marks, Parentheses, Italics, and Underlines

LESSON SUMMARY

It is helpful to know how to write dialogue, insert a parenthetical comment, and editorialize in your writing. Learn the proper way to do these things in this lesson.

Quotation Marks

Quotation marks are used in writing to show someone's exact words, or dialogue. This word-for-word account is called a **direct quotation**. To set the direct quotation apart, you need to use opening and ending quotation marks: " and ".

> ### ⮑ TIP
>
> When attributing quotations, as with any dialogue, choose interesting verbs. Constant use of "he said" or "she said" can become tedious. Use a variety of synonyms, like "he announced," "they replied," "he acknowledged," "they reported," or "she queried."

If someone just *refers* to someone else's words, this is called an **indirect quotation**, which does NOT require quotation marks.

Example:
Margaret said that Jason from IT told her to change her password.

Quotation marks also are not used in recording someone's thoughts.

Example:
Margaret thought she should choose a password that's easy to remember.

We sometimes put quotation marks around a word (or words) to stress its meaning or to convey uncertainty or misgivings about its validity to readers.

Example:
It escapes me why Victor, a Wall Street broker, was asked to speak to our Lifeguard Association as an "expert" on rescue techniques.

⤷ TIP

Here are some helpful guidelines for using quotation marks:

- Capitalize the first word of a direct quotation if it is the first word of the quotation or starts the sentence in which it is quoted.
- Always place periods and commas inside the end quotes.
- Place question marks and exclamation marks inside the end quotes only if they are part of the quotation. Otherwise, place them after the end quotes.

   Examples:
   Nancy whined, "I am so hungry!"
   Did you hear her say, "I can't eat another bite"?

- Always place colons and semicolons outside the end quote.
- Place a comma before the opening quotes when the quote is preceded by words that imply speaking, such as *said*, *stated*, *replied*, and *cried*.

   Example:
   Cosmos whispered, "I can't see—please move over."

- When a quote is interrupted, enclose each part in quotation marks. Place a comma inside the first end quotes, and then follow the interrupting words with a comma before adding the second opening quotes.

   Example:
   "The first quarter's numbers are in," remarked Ted, "and they look very encouraging!"

Note that *and* at the beginning of the second part of the quote is not capitalized because it is not starting a new sentence but continuing the first.

Practice

Place quotation marks, commas, and end marks in the following sentences, and change to caps as needed, or note that they are correct as written.

1. "oh my goodness" she exclaimed, startled by the unexpected fire alarm.

2. When Bobby brewer the superstar player struck out for the third time in a row the stadium erupted in angry shouts of booooo

3. The label on the paint can said the color was pacific turquoise but it looked more like regular green to me

4. "Can you put this away for me" she asked tossing me the stack of files

5. "Bad dog" Evelyn yelled, while grover a yorkshire terrier, lowered his head and slunk away from the damaged couch.

6. This is the best catered lunch I've ever eaten

7. Our boat the *mademoiselle Marie* was put away for the winter at dockside marina.

8. Argus's annual review said that he was "too distracted" in meetings and should pay more attention so he is aware of company policies.

9. Wow thanks he yelled joyfully after realizing his co-worker had decorated his cubicle for his birthday.

10. Which account is the Jorgenson family's

Parentheses

Parentheses are used to provide extra or incidental information within or at the end of a sentence. The information inside the parentheses is called a **parenthetical comment**.

Example:

Ron Kenny wound up with the Salesperson of the Year Award (remember how he struggled at the beginning of the year?).

Note that even if you take the parenthetical comment out of the sentence, it still makes sense.

Parentheses also set off dates and page numbers within sentences or in citations in some styles of academic writing.

Examples:

Information regarding the migration of Monarch butterflies can be found in Chapter 22 (pages 97–113).

In a famous study of Jane Austen (1775–1817) and her many literary accomplishments (Dawson, 1989) . . .

Parentheses can be used for itemizing numbers or letters:

Please write your (1) name, (2) address, and (3) DOB.

Please write your (a) name, (b) address, and (c) DOB.

⇨ TIP

If your parenthetical comment is part of the whole sentence, do not put a period or other end mark inside the parentheses. But if the note is a complete sentence, put a punctuation mark inside the parentheses.

Parentheses are also used for providing, or defining, abbreviations.

Examples:
There has been recent news from the National Aeronautics and Space Administration (NASA) . . . .
The Federal Communications Commission (FCC) has issued a new . . . .

Finally, parentheses can be used to indicate an alternative form of a written term.

Examples:
Before printing, carefully select the page(s) you need.
Write the name(s) on the form and submit.

Practice

Determine where parentheses should be placed in the following sentences.

11. Bob Flenderson a famous anthropologist returned from his work in the Amazon rain forest last week.

12. Anya moved to the United States when she was 17 which was in 1996.

13. The Florida Gators' record 16–2 is the best in their conference.

14. Did you know that the escalator is out of order and has been for more than a week?

15. Those doughnuts are amazing I ate at least three of them.

Italics and Underlines

When writing by hand, italicizing words is difficult, so we underline them instead. In printing and word processing, we can use either one (although underscores are uncommon). Just remember to be consistent. Don't use one and then another for the same purpose in the same text.

Italicize (or underline) the titles of long works such as books, long poems, magazines, newspapers, or movies.

Examples:

James Michener's *Chesapeake*

The New Yorker
Robert Frost's *Collected Poems*

James Michener's Chesapeake
The New Yorker
Robert Frost's Collected Poems

Set off shorter works such as stories, songs, short poems, and articles with quotation marks rather than italics or underlines.

Italicize foreign words in your writing.

Example:

The handsome man said, "*Ciao bella*," when he left the table.

When you want to emphasize a particular word, italicize (or underline) it. The following chart shows how emphasizing different words in a sentence can change the meaning completely.

SAME SENTENCE, FOUR DIFFERENT MEANINGS	
I like your shoes.	It is I, and only I, who likes them
I *like* your shoes.	Don't love them, just like them
I like *your* shoes.	No one else's but yours
I like your *shoes*.	Not your outfit or your hair, but your shoes

Practice

Identify the words and phrases that need to be italicized (or underlined) in the following sentences.

16. We finally got tickets to see Cat on a Hot Tin Roof on Broadway.

17. Our cruise ship was called the Jewel of the Seven Seas.

18. The Daily Show, 60 Minutes, and the Today show are my favorite current-events TV shows.

19. The keys for the letters a, q, and p are sticking on my keyboard.

20. He has a certain je ne sais quois that draws me to him.

Answers

1. "Oh, my goodness!" she exclaimed, startled by the unexpected fireworks.
2. When Bobby Brewer, the superstar player, struck out for the third time in a row, the stadium erupted in angry shouts of "Booooo!"
3. The label on the paint can said the color was "Pacific Turquoise," but it looked more like regular green to me.
4. "Can you put this away for me?" she asked, tossing me the box of crackers.
5. "Bad dog!" Evelyn yelled, while Grover, a Yorkshire terrier, lowered his head and slunk away from the damaged couch.
6. This is the best French toast I've ever eaten!
7. Our boat, the *Mademoiselle Marie*, was put away for the winter at Dockside Marina.
8. This sentence is correct as is.
9. "Wow, thanks!" he yelled joyfully after finding his new bike parked in front of the Christmas tree.
10. Which house is the Jorgenson family's?
11. Bob Flenderson (a famous anthropologist) returned from his work in the Amazon rain forest last week.
12. Anya moved to the United States when she was 17 (which was in 1996).
13. The Florida Gators' record (16–2) is the best in their conference.
14. Did you know that the escalator is out of order (and has been for more than a week)?
15. Those doughnuts are amazing (I ate at least three of them).
16. *Cat on a Hot Tin Roof*
17. *Jewel of the Seven Seas*
18. *The Daily Show*, *60 Minutes*, and the *Today* show
19. *a*, *q*, and *p*
20. *je ne sais quois*

POSTTEST ▶

Now that you have spent a good deal of time improving your grammar skills, take this posttest to see how much you have learned. Take as much time as you need to finish the test, and then read through the answer explanations at the end of the chapter, and tally your score.

If you took the pretest at the beginning of the book, you can compare what you knew then with what you know now. Check your score on this posttest against your score on the pretest. If this score is much higher, congratulations—you have profited noticeably from your hard work. If your score shows little improvement, you may want to review certain chapters, especially if you see a pattern to the kinds of questions you missed. Whatever your score, keep this book handy for review and reference whenever you are unsure of a grammatical rule.

Posttest

1. Find and correct the capitalization errors in these sentences.
- I was delighted to see katelyn and andrew last saturday Afternoon.
- the spanish Test on tuesday was hard.
- martin's Journey to mount rushmore in keystone, south dakota, was unforgettable.
- charlie couldn't sleep because his Puppy, casper, whined all night long.

2. Circle the nouns that are pluralized correctly.

televisions	flys	mouses
womans	tooths	analyses
ferries	deers	igloos
knifes	pluses	volcanoes

3. Circle the hyphenated nouns that are spelled correctly.

frees-for-all	not-for-profits
fathers-in-law	voice-overs

4. Circle the nouns that have been made possessive correctly.

horse's	ants's	doctors'
kittens's	bus'	teachers'
children's	classes'	Max's
bands's	child's	class's

5. Circle the pairs of antecedents and pronouns that agree.

Matt/her	fishermen/they	Paul and I/we
mice/they	each/we	deer/it
workers/it	everyone/they	deer/they
Cheryl/she	company/it	
you and I/we	player/we	

6. Circle the correct form of lay/lie in each sentence.

Sammy usually (lays, lies) his schoolbooks on his desk.

This mysterious trunk has (lain, laid) untouched in this attic for decades.

The shopkeeper (laid, lain) his apron on the counter before locking up for the night.

7. Circle the correct form of sit/set in each sentence.

Janice is (setting, sitting) the table before her guests arrive.

Jim (sat, set) down in the comfortable chair and took a short nap.

We had (set, sat) our glasses of lemonade on the orange coasters beside us.

8. Circle the correct word in each sentence.

"Mom, (can, may) I sell some of this old jewelry online?" I asked.

He answered every question on the exam correctly (accept, except) the last one.

Marcy, Chris, and I (hanged, hung) out at the mall almost all day Saturday.

9. Place the correct indefinite article in front of each term.

____ hen	____ hour-long lecture
____ honor	____ universe
____ one-car family	____ wristwatch
____ orthodontist	____ upperclassman
____ honeybee	____ elegant dinner
____ orangutan	____ underwater city
____ ozone layer	____ opinion
____ umbrella	

10. Determine which form of comparative or superlative adjective best completes each sentence.

> The (cooler, coolest) day yet this week was Wednesday, and it was 97 degrees.
>
> Yuck! This rock is (slimy, slimier) than the other one.
>
> My shoes are the (narrower, narrowest) of all.

11. Circle the correct form of the comparative and superlative adverbs in the following sentences.

> Of the three jockeys, Marco rode (more cautiously, most cautiously) during the race.
>
> My flight from L.A. to Tucson seemed (longer, longest) than the one from Tucson to New York.
>
> People said my coconut custard pie tasted good; in fact, Sam said it tasted (better, best) than his mom's!

12. Rewrite each sentence so that the misplaced modifiers are properly placed.

> Having been burned to a crisp, the chef threw the roast into the sink.
>
> Crocks of onion soup were served to the guests dripping with cheese.
>
> At the age of five, Kerry's parents brought her to Walt Disney World.

13. Identify the simple subject in the following sentences.

> Animals that sleep during the day and are awake at night are called nocturnal.
>
> Artificial intelligence is used not only in games, but for medical purposes as well.
>
> Please stop.
>
> Most liked it, although some did not.
>
> Although he lives on his own, Mike still likes coming home once in a while.

14. Identify the verb that correctly completes the following sentences.

Bacon and eggs (are, is) the favorite dish of many people who stop at our diner.

Kara and Maria (try, tries) out for the community theater's musical production every year.

Science fiction or mystery (are, is) the only choice of genre left to choose from for my report.

15. Identify the verb that will agree with the indefinite pronouns in the following sentences.

Everyone (go, goes) to the prom each year.

Something (need, needs) to be done about that leak.

While each (prefers, prefer) to eat yogurt, the time of day it's eaten varies widely.

16. Determine which pronoun best fits for proper pronoun-antecedent agreement in each sentence.

The group took _____ yearly retreat to Maine.

Everyone carefully opened _____ package.

The puppy wagged _____ tail eagerly when it saw the mailman at the door.

17. Determine whether each group of words is an independent or a subordinate clause.

as I said

I am learning ballroom dancing

here are some for you

well, I should say so

that's life

stop that

18. Identify the simple, compound, complex, and compound-complex sentences.
    a. Some citizens voted in the town election, but many did not.
    b. If you want to make mashed potatoes, just add butter and milk to the boiled potatoes and mash until creamy.
    c. Put your folded laundry away, please.
    d. Because Jill was late, she missed the introductory overview of the entire workshop.

19. Add punctuation where necessary in the following sentences.
    On April 12 1861 the Civil War began with the battle at Fort Sumter
    The dentists hygienists and staff threw a surprise party for him
    Would you consider using Benjis or Jesss racket for now

20. Correctly place quotation marks, commas, and end marks in the following sentences.
    It's not easy to memorize all of the mathematical formulas for algebra stated Mrs. Shapiro but we'll accomplish that by the year's end
    Would you make my steak sandwich without onions please asked Harry
    I began Courtney am not the only girl who feels that way

Answers

If you miss any of the following questions, you may refer to the designated lesson for further explanation.

1.
   - I was delighted to see Katelyn and Andrew last Saturday afternoon.
   - The Spanish test on Tuesday was hard.
   - Martin's journey to Mount Rushmore in Keystone, South Dakota, was unforgettable.
   - Charlie couldn't sleep because his puppy, Casper, whined all night long.

2. The correct answers are *televisions, analyses, ferries, igloos, pluses,* and *volcanoes.* Of the other options, *flys* should change the *-ys* to *-ies. Mouse, woman, tooth,* and *deer* are all irregular nouns, with the plurals *mice, women, teeth,* and *deer.* And finally, remember that *-ife* words like *knife* become plural with the ending *-ives.* (Lesson 1)

3. The correct answers are *not-for-profits, fathers-in-law,* and *voice-overs.* These hyphenated compound nouns add the *-s* to the word that changes in number. *Frees-for-all* incorrectly pluralizes the adjective, not the count noun. (Lesson 1)

4. The correct answers are *horse's, doctors', teachers', children's, classes', Max's, child's,* and *class's.* (Lesson 1)

5. The correct answers are:

mice/they	*fishermen/they*	*deer/it*
Cheryl/she	*company/it*	*deer/they*
you and I/we	*Paul and I/we*	

   Mice, you and I, fishermen, and *Paul and I* are all plural, so they take plural pronouns. *Cheryl* is a female name, so *she* is the correct pronoun. *Workers* is plural, so the singular pronoun *it* is incorrect. *Companies* are not people, so they take the neutral pronoun *it. Deer* is trickier but is correct in both instances—because *deer* is an irregular noun, the plural and singular are the same. (Lesson 2)

6. The correct answers are *lays*, *lain*, and *laid*. The first and third sentences have instances of objects being placed somewhere, which means that the correct verb will be versions of to *lay*. The second sentence requires the past participle of to *lie* (to be situated). (Lesson 3)

7. The correct answers are *setting*, *sat*, and *set*. To *set* means to place objects, like Janice is doing, and we are doing with our glasses. To *sit* means to *be seated* or *be situated* in a particular place, as Jim was. (Lesson 3)

8. The correct answers are *may*, *except*, and *hung*. In the first sentence, the speaker is asking for permission, not trying to determine whether something is possible, so *may* is the correct choice. In the second sentence, you already know that he answered all the other questions. That suggests that the last question is different, and therefore you're looking for *except*. In the third sentence, that the speaker is spending time with friends suggests that the circumstances have nothing to do with the gallows (*hanged*), so you can go with the irregular past participle of to *hang*: *hung*. (Lesson 3)

9. The correct answers are:
> *a hen*
> *an honor*
> *a one-car family*
> *an orthodontist*
> *a honeybee*
> *an orangutan*
> *an ozone layer*
> *an umbrella*
> *an hour-long lecture*
> *a universe*
> *a wristwatch*
> *an upperclassman*
> *an elegant dinner*
> *an underwater city*
> *an opinion*

As you may recall, the quickest way to determine indefinite articles is to sound out the nouns they modify. Words that start with a vowel (or a vowel sound) call for *an*. The letter *h* makes things tricky—but remember that if the *h* is silent, like in *honorable* or *hour*, go with *an*; if the *h* is not silent, like in *hen*, go with *a*. Words that start with a consonant (or sound like they start with a consonant, like the *w* sound of *one*) call for *a*. (Lesson 5)

10. The correct answers are *coolest*, *slimier*, and *narrowest*. Remember that when it comes to comparatives and superlatives, use *-est* (superlative ending) when more than two things are being compared (like days of the week or all shoes). When only two things are being compared, like two rocks, the adjective is comparative rather than superlative, so *-er* is the proper suffix. (Lesson 5)

11. The correct answers are *most cautiously*, *longer*, and *better*. When more than two items are being compared (as with the three jockeys in the first sentence), choose the superlative (*most cautiously*). If two items are being compared (as with the two flights in the second sentence and my pie/Sam's mom's pie in the third sentence), choose the comparative adverb (*longer* and *better*, respectively). (Lesson 5)

12. The correct answers are:

> The chef threw the roast, which was burned to a crisp, into the sink.
>
> Crocks of onion soup dripping with cheese were served to the guests.
>
> When Kerry was five, her parents brought her to Disney World.

In the first sentence, you need to make clear that it was the roast, not the chef, that was burned to a crisp. In the second sentence, is the soup dripping with cheese, or are the guests? Were Kerry's parents five years old, or was Kerry? By making sure that modifiers are placed near the nouns they're modifying, you make the sentence and its meaning much clearer. (Lesson 7)

13. The simple subjects are *animals, artificial intelligence, [you], most,* and *Mike.* The subject is the person or object that is performing the action of the sentence. What is called nocturnal? *Animals.* What is used for games and medical purposes? *Artificial intelligence.* Who should stop? *You* (or rather, the person to whom the speaker is talking). Who liked it? *Most.* Who lives on his own and comes home once in a while? *Mike.* To help you identify the subject of a sentence, locate the nouns or pronouns, and determine whether they tell you what the sentence is about. (Lesson 8)

14. The correct answers are *is, try,* and *is. Bacon and eggs* may seem plural, but they really work together as one noun (a dish). In the second sentence, *Kara and Maria* (two separate people) are plural, so they take the plural present-tense verb *try.* In the third sentence, the *or* tells you that you are dealing with a single subject (either *science fiction* or *mystery,* not both). (Lesson 8)

15. The correct answers are *goes, needs,* and *prefers.* Look closely at the subjects of the sentences (which, in these cases, are indefinite pronouns). *Everyone, something,* and *each* are all singular, so they take the singular present-tense third-person verb (*goes, needs, prefers*). (Lesson 8)

16. The correct answers are *its, his or her,* and *its.* In the first sentence, the subject *the group* is singular, and therefore calls for the singular possessive *its.* In the second sentence, the subject *everyone* is singular—but from the context of the sentence, you can't tell whether the people involved are male or female, so you should go with *his or her.* In the third sentence, the subject is singular, but a *puppy* is an animal, so it takes the neutral possessive *its.* (Lesson 8)

17. The correct answers are:

> ***as I said:*** *subordinate clause*
> ***I am learning ballroom dancing:*** *independent clause*
> ***here are some for you:*** *independent clause*
> ***well, I should say so:*** *independent clause*
> ***that's life:*** *independent clause*
> ***stop that:*** *independent clause*

The best way to determine whether something is an independent clause is to see if it can stand as a sentence on its own. If the clause leaves you hanging (*as I said* . . . what did you say?), then it's a subordinate clause that relies on an independent clause to tell you what's going on in the sentence. Independent clauses have a clear subject and predicate. (Lesson 9)

18. The correct answers are:
   a. compound
   b. compound-complex
   c. simple
   d. complex

Sentence **a** contains two subjects (*some citizens* and *many*) and two predicates (*voted in the town election* and *did not*), so it is a compound sentence. Sentence **b** contains two independent clauses (*just add butter and milk to the boiled potatoes* and *mash until creamy*) and a subordinate clause (*if you want to make mashed potatoes*), which makes it a compound-complex sentence. Sentence **c** has a single subject (the implied *you*) and a single predicate (*put your folded laundry away, please*); it is one independent clause, so it is a simple sentence. Sentence **d** has one subordinate clause (*because Jill was late*) and one independent clause (*she missed the introductory overview of the entire workshop*), so it is a complex sentence. (Lesson 11)

19. The correct answers are:

> *On April 12, 1861, the Civil War began with the battle at Fort Sumter.*
>
> *The dentist's hygienists and staff threw a surprise party for him.*
>
> *Would you consider using Benji's or Jess's racket for now?*

In the first sentence, use a comma to separate the day and the year, and add a comma after *1861* to set the year off with commas and to conclude the introductory phrase. As always, you should make sure that your sentence ends with proper punctuation; this sentence isn't a question or an exclamation, so it ends with a period. In the second sentence, make sure it's clear that the hygienists and staff belong to the dentist, and place the possessive apostrophe accordingly (after determining whether the sentence is about a single dentist or a group of dentists). And again, make sure that the end punctuation is in place—in this case (a common statement), it's a period. In the third sentence, the racket belongs to the Benji or Jess, so you need possessive apostrophes. Double-*s* words can be tricky, but three *s*'s in a row tell you that something is wrong—and given that *Jess* is a singular noun, you know that it should get the singular, possessive -'s. This sentence is also missing end punctuation. The helping verb *would* at the beginning of the sentence tells you that a question is being asked, so the correct end punctuation is a question mark. (Lessons 12–15)

20. The correct answers are:

> "It's not easy to memorize all of the mathematical formulas for algebra," stated Mrs. Shapiro, "but we'll accomplish that by the year's end."
>
> "Would you make my steak sandwich without onions, please?" asked Harry.
>
> "I," began Courtney, "am not the only girl who feels that way."

In these sentences, it's important to read through and separate the parts of the sentences to make it clear who is talking and what they are saying. In the first sentence, *stated Mrs. Shapiro* tells you that it's a direct quote, but the *we'll* that follows suggests that the quote starts up again after pausing in the middle to tell you who is speaking. So it's important to set off the middle section (*stated Mrs. Shapiro*) with commas and to be sure that each section of the full quote begins and ends with quotation marks. The second sentence ends with *asked Harry*, telling you that everything that comes before that point is part of Harry's question. In addition to placing the quotation marks correctly so that you know what Harry is asking, it's also key to add the correct end punctuation to the quote: a question mark. The third sentence, like the first, pauses within the quote to let you know who is speaking, so it's important to figure out what Courtney is saying directly and how she is saying it. (Lessons 12–15)

ADDITIONAL ONLINE PRACTICE

Using the code below, you'll be able to log in and access additional online practice materials!

Your free online practice access code is:
LELCOLT069

Follow these simple steps to redeem your code:

- Go to **www.learningexpresshub.com/affiliate** and have your access code handy.

If you're a new user:

- Click the **New user? Register here** button and complete the registration form to create your account and access your products.
- Be sure to enter your unique access code only once. If you have multiple access codes, you can enter them all—just use a comma to separate each code.
- The next time you visit, simply click the **Returning user? Sign in** button and enter your username and password.
- Do not re-enter previously redeemed access code. Any products you previously accessed are saved in the **My Account** section on the site. Entering a previously redeemed access code will result in an error message.

If you're a returning user:

- Click the **Returning user? Sign in** button, enter your username and password, and click **Sign In**.
- You will automatically be brought to the **My Account** page to access your products.
- Do not re-enter previously redeemed access code. Any products you previously accessed are saved in the **My Account** section on the site. Entering a previously redeemed access code will result in an error message.

If you're a returning user with a new access code:

- Click the **Returning user? Sign in** button, enter your username, password, and new access code, and click **Sign In**.
- If you have multiple access codes, you can enter them all—just use a comma to separate each code.
- Do not re-enter previously redeemed access code. Any products you previously accessed are saved in the **My Account** section on the site. Entering a previously redeemed access code will result in an error message.

If you have any questions, please contact LearningExpress Customer Support at LXHub@LearningExpressHub.com. All inquiries will be responded to within a 24-hour period during our normal business hours: 9 A.M.–5 P.M. Eastern Time. Thank you!